THE BETRAYAL OF THE POOR
The Transformation of Community Action

STEPHEN M. ROSE

SCHENKMAN PUBLISHING COMPANY
Cambridge, Massachusetts 02138

Foreword

Stephen M. Rose's, *The Betrayal of the Poor: The Transformation of Community Action,* is one of the most challenging pieces of analysis to come out of the experience of the local community action programs of the "war on poverty." The author concludes from his analysis that the very agencies in the local community which the community action program was to stimulate to change—agencies which often perceived the new program as a threat—were nevertheless able to absorb the impact of the action programs and to mold these programs to fit their own operational requirements and styles.

The author documents the important emphasis placed on institutional change and a redistribution of power by the Presidential Task Force on Urban Areas, which developed the guidelines for the community action strategy. He examines in depth the implications of the difference between diagnosing the causes of poverty as lying in the pathological characteristics of individual poor people and in an alleged "culture of poverty," or diagnosing the causes as lying in an institutional order so structured as to produce poverty as systematically and as inevitably as it produces affluence. The former diagnosis would point to a strategy of increasing agency services that would bear on inadequate individuals, while the latter would call for changing the institutional structure to equalize opportunity for the poor, organizing the poor as a self-conscious group alert to its own interests and actively pursuing them, and transferring some share of decision-making power to disadvantaged groups.

The Presidential Task Force was clear that both major strategies were needed—an expansion of "services," particularly in the field of education, and a social action program which would bring about institutional change.

Yet in his analysis of the project components of the community action program in twenty cities, using data gathered in the Brandeis study of Community Representation in Community Action Programs, Rose finds that less than 3% of these projects were in any way designed to organize the poor, to transfer power, or to change the institutional structure. Furthermore, the greater the number of local agencies which participated in setting up the local community action programs, the less was the likelihood that anything but an out-and-out service strategy based on the assumptions of individual pathology and the "culture of the poor" would take place. The result was that although in many cities more or less conventional agency services were expanded or improved, virtually no impact hit the environment which produced the poverty in the first place. In this sense, although he does not suggest a "conspiracy," the author asserts that the poor were betrayed. At the same time, agencies, whose inability to deal effectively with the problem had been a major cause for the poverty program, ended up by, in effect, finding themselves able to use this program to expand their own budgets.

In a final chapter, Rose comments on these paradoxical facts, and explains the paradox by documenting the point that the Presidential Task Force, though convinced of the necessity for a social action strategy, nevertheless chose a means of implementing the program through coordinative effort by existing agencies. It was utopian, he asserts, to expect that these agencies would voluntarily change their programs in the direction hoped for by the Task Force. The evidence from this study, he concludes, indicates that the sought-for collaboration between existing agencies served to thwart reform and innovation rather than to stimulate them. This occurred through a process in which power, perception, and program were mutually reinforcing and constituted an effective barrier to significant change.

Roland L. Warren

Acknowledgments

I CAN think of three sources of stimulation and encouragement which influenced my intellectual development and the preparation of this study. First, there was my family. Thanks which cannot be expressed adequately are due my wife for her continual support and devotion during a long period where other obligations could have competed for my attention. Second, there were two true teachers whose continued stimulation, confrontation, and concern contributed not only to whatever substantive knowledge I possess, but to my ability to utilize it: Roland Warren and Norman Kurtz made my experience at the Heller School an enviable one in their attention and consideration for me and whatever work happened to engage me. Third, there were the numerous scholars (both those publicly acknowledged and those whom I privately respected) whose ideas, writings, and suggestions have accumulated in my mind over the years. For those whose work has been formalized, credit is given in the footnotes and bibliography of this study; for the others, who go unspecified, an anonymous citation must suffice. Other sources of motivation, less formal and more idiosyncratic, include several students who participated with me in several seminars and lengthy discussions: Carl Milofsky, Lee Friedman, Jo Holz, and Benjamin Kerner come immediately to my mind. Other students, low income people who attended a class at the University of Maine in Portland, gave me considerable motivation to continue work similar to this study by their interest in the material and their indications that its content was useful to them in their attempts to create an authentic social policy.

Thanks are also extended to my Dissertation Committee composed of Sanford Kravitz, William Gamson, and Gunnar Dybwad, in addition to Roland Warren and Norman Kurtz.

David Austin, the Study Director of the Citizen Participation Project, was most cooperative and helpful in allowing me the use of the data and in helping me clarify some of the information presented in Chapter VII. And thanks are owed to Edwina Mallek for her patience and perseverance in preparation of the manuscript and to Maureen Power for her critical reading of it; both their contributions have been most helpful.

Stephen M. Rose

Table of Contents

CHAPTER I

Introduction

On March 16, 1964 President Lyndon Baines Johnson sent a "Message on Poverty" to the Congress of the United States. In part, he said "There are millions of Americans—one-fifth of our people—who have not shared in the abundance which has been granted to most of us, and on whom the gates of opportunity have been closed."[1] This statement marked official recognition of the existence of broadspread deprivation in a nation characterized by an accelerating gross national product, a sustained period of economic growth, and conspicuous consumption. To be sure, the poor have been among us and have been documented for several years by various governmental agencies including the Bureau of the Census, the Bureau of Labor Statistics, the Social Security Administration, and the Department of Agriculture, but as a group the poor remained ignored in the official interests and policies of America throughout the 1950's.

In the early years of the next decade, a growing awareness of the existence of poverty and discrimination was forced upon the nation by the Civil Rights Movement. In challenging the laws and customs of local areas as well as our national policies, the Civil Rights Movement changed the focus of the American public from apathetic acceptance of poor people to some recognition of the circumstances in which they lived. These circumstances were made clear to the late President Kennedy in his primary election campaign tour through West Virginia, but their plight did not emerge as a major public issue in the presidential campaign of 1960. According to Lewis Coser,

Historically, the poor emerge when society elects to recognize poverty as a special status and assigns specific persons to that category. The fact that some people may privately consider themselves poor is sociologically irrelevant. What is sociologically relevent is poverty as a socially recognized condition, as a social status.[2]

This recognition seems to have come upon America by 1962: Fortune Magazine in 1960 had published an issue entitled *America In The 60's* which forecast that deprivation would soon cease to exist, that only 3.6 million families had incomes under $2,000 per year; anything beyond that was not considered poverty.[3] Only two years later Michael Harrington's book, *The Other America,* was published and further dramatized the personal plight of the poor. According to Coser,

The deprived in America now were seen as constituting about 25 percent of the population, all of whom deserved assistance. The number of objectively deprived is not likely to have changed appreciably between the complacent fifties and the self-critical sixties, but the extent of perceived deprivation changed drastically. As a consequence, what appeared as a peripheral problem only a few years ago suddenly assumes considerable national salience.[4]

There is little question about the emergence of the poor as a relevant social and political category during the early 1960's. The mass media, aided by popularized social science, contributed to the national reawakening. Books about the poor such as those written by Michael Harrington and Oscar Lewis became best sellers during this time. Both the President's Council of Economic Advisers and the Chamber of Commerce undertook large-scale studies of poverty and made public their results. Whatever the reason for the homage paid to poverty and its unfortunate inhabitants, the range of views on the subject was broad. Simultaneous with the rediscovery of the poor was a proliferation of social policy recommendations and social programming proposals for the alleviation of poverty. The suggestions for action were often proposed within implicit conceptual frameworks regarding the position of the poor in an otherwise affluent America. At times, such assumptions were made clear and programs were forged around them; for example, the Grey Areas Program of the Ford Foundation. Poverty as a public problem, as a part of American society, became a part of the social reality of the 1960's.

The author's commitment to the need for revolution in the social structure of American society and concern with how the need was manifest in the rhetoric of the anti-poverty program led eventually to this study. The subsequent failure of the national poverty program and the evaporation of public concern about the poverty problem raise important questions of both an intellectual and political nature. This study will focus on the intellectual aspect, examining the selection of a definition for the Community Action Program from among three alternative ideal types and following the effects of this orientation through to the implementation stage in local communities across the nation.

The remainder of this chapter will examine varying conceptions of the problem of poverty, and related strategies for social intervention. Further, the analytical strategy for the remainder of the study will be described, including discussion of the theoretical framework, the source of the data, and the methodology.

ALTERNATIVE PERSPECTIVES ON THE PROBLEM

Explanations of the problem of poverty range on a continuum which has as its criterion the degree to which either the individual or the society in which he lives is portrayed as responsible for his being poor. At one extreme can be found the notion that the condition of poverty is brought about by its inhabitants because of their own basic defects, deviant values, and/or immorality. Related to this position are perceptions of

poverty as a cycle or an intergenerational problem existing
within a distinct subculture in American life. Barry Goldwater,
a Presidential candidate in 1964, illustrates this view in the
following statements: "I'm tired of professional chiselers walk-
ing up and down the streets who don't work and have no intention of working." [5] "The fact is that most people who have no
skills have no education for the same reason—low intelligence
or low ambition." [6] Galbraith's concept of "case poverty"
approximates this position:

Case poverty is commonly and properly related to some characteristics of the individuals so afflicted. Nearly everyone else has mastered
his environment; this proves that it is not intractable. But some
quality peculiar to the individual or family involved — mental deficiency, bad health, inability to adapt to the discipline of modern
economic life, excessive procreation, alcohol, insufficient education,
or perhaps a combination of these several handicaps have kept these
individuals from participating in the general well-being. [7]

At the other extreme are perceptions of poverty which reject
both the subcultural and intergenerational concepts of the
problem, and emphasize structural causes. One such structural view is Hyman Lumer's: "Basically, poverty today stems
from the drive of giant corporations for maximum profits,
which means not only holding wages down and not only sweat-
ing extra profits out of the small farmers, the small businessmen, the Negro people and other groups, but also holding
government welfare expenditures to a minimum." [8] Other
analysts of this persuasion take a different part of the existing
social system, such as the economy, the schools or current welfare practices, and weave an explanation around that one-
dimensional variable. Some writers leave the causal explanation of the problem implicit in their recommendations for
programmatic action to eliminate poverty. Both the explanations offered and the policies suggested reflect a growing

involvement of social scientists with the issues posed by the existence of poverty in our society.

By 1960 the presence of academicians in the government as staff members and consultants was not a new phenomenon in America. But the direct influence on social policy by these people had rarely been so visible. The impact was felt in two ways, and, while this matter will be dealt with below, it is appropriate here to acknowledge the impact of the academicians on both the perceptions of the poverty problem and the strategies for resolving it. Such "activist social scientists" were the concern of a recent book by Daniel Moynihan,[9] who imputed to those responsible for the development of the community action concept the responsibility for increasing social conflict in America and diverting the nation from its proper course, one based on guaranteed full employment and some form of income maintenance. Other critics attacked either the research-experimental nature of the programs initiated by the President's Committee on Juvenile Delinquency and Youth Crime or the lack of research and planning in the Community Action Program of the Office of Economic Opportunity. A review of suggested program approaches, as well as of the range of perspectives about the cause of the problem, will enable the reader to detect the bases for vast differences of opinion.

Almost all action proposals carry with them the assumption that poverty is the absence of some vitally needed resource: for some that resource is money, for others it is housing, for others it is power, etc. If we construct a continuum of action proposals which parallels the continuum we used to look at conceptual perspectives on the problem—with the individual as the focus on one end and with the social structure as the focus on the other—a wide range of programmatic options can be classified for examination. At the individualistic end, programmatic recommendations consist of such projects as training to improve character or work habits, social services and rehabilitation programs, or remedial education. At some point along the continuum would be those programs and policies geared to increase transfer payments to different categories of the poor, to train the poor for existing jobs (including subsidies to businesses which undertake such programs), to accelerate national economic growth, to improve labor markets (by giving relocation aid, improving information on employment opportunities, and increasing unemployment benefits), and to give loans to small businesses.

At the other pole, oriented to the social system, the programmatic alternatives would include organizing low income people for political purposes, promoting the participation of service users in the policy-making bodies of the service systems, creating new types of jobs for the poor, and developing new organizations of the poor to compete with traditional agencies for resources. This range is broad and parallels the range of perceptions about the poverty problem itself. Not surprisingly, conflicts between advocates of the different positions arose. Each position regarding solutions to the problem represented an attempt to maximize the belief system underlying that position. The operationalization of these values and derived perceptions of the problem, translating them from paper into an organizational reality through planning and political negotiation (at a later point, the author will question whether such a distinction can be made), formed the stage on which the national crusade to end poverty was acted out.

During the early 1960's, a period heightened by liberal optimism, solutions to the poverty problem appeared credible. Action systems within local communities began to move beyond the boundaries of the local community or the "horizontal" system to seek funds from foundations and government agencies to resolve local problems. The changing lines of financing such programs, specifically the inclusion of financial resources from extra-community units, and the growing concern with

coordination of efforts in eliminating social ills also brought
a commitment to rational social planning. University faculty
members joined the New Frontier or became consultants to it
in growing numbers. They formed the core of the new planners, focusing on maximizing community resources, making
decisions about program coordination and innovation, allo-
cating funds, and involving local residents in the design of
programs.

The period described certainly can be seen as a time of oscillation. Sometimes it was felt that the enormity of the problems
confronted could be encountered successfully; at other times,
the very ideas which were so stimulating in the plans failed
to produce the changes expected. Unfortunately, it appears
that the social scientist-turned-social planner did not take the
time to evaluate his initial efforts, to regroup, to question his
concept of the problems before him. In contrast, he was swept
up in the social dynamics of the time, moving from one oasis
of proclaimed innovation and creativity to the next, from the
President's Committee to Community Mental Health, or to the
Anti-Poverty Program, or to Model Cities. In a time when the
very basis for the contribution of comprehensive social planning to the resolution of urban problems should have been
questioned, given its overall performance in the Ford Foundation Grey Areas Program, the Community Action Program,
Model Cities, and others, the planners have failed to examine
where they have gone wrong. This study proposes to take
advantage of the insulation provided by the university; its
author chooses to resist the impetus to develop new planning
models for new programs, selecting instead the examination
of one planned program developed conceptually by men experienced in urban politics and social problems—the Community Action Program of the Office of Economic Opportunity.

The Community Action Program was cast as a point of
mobilization and coordination of local resources for mounting
an attack on poverty as defined by each community. John

Wofford, staff assistant to the deputy director of the Program, describes the effort in the following way: "In the Community Action Program, poverty was to be defined, its causes were to be specified, and solutions were to be proposed—not by the federal government, but by local communities throughout the nation." [10] According to the Economic Opportunity Act of 1964, the local Community Action Agency (CAA) was to serve as the organization which would stimulate, develop, coordinate and conduct programs consistent with the mandate. Specifically, the legislation states, "The purpose of this part (Title IIA) is to provide stimulation and incentive for urban and rural communities to mobilize their resources to combat poverty through community action programs." The legislation continues, defining a community action program as one—

(1) which mobilizes and utilizes resources, public or private, of any urban or rural, or combined urban and rural, geographical area (referred to in this part as a "community"), including but not limited to a State, metropolitan area, county, city, town, multi-city unit, or multi-county unit in an attack on poverty;

(2) which provides services, assistance, and other activities of sufficient scope and size to give promise of progress towards elimination of poverty or a cause or causes of poverty through developing employment opportunities, improving human performance, motivation, and productivity, or bettering the condition under which people live, learn, and work;

(3) which is developed, conducted, and administered with the maximum feasible participation of residents of the areas and members of the groups served; and

(4) which is conducted, administered, and coordinated by a public or private nonprofit agency (other than a political party), or a combination thereof.[11]

The various interpretations of this legislation, particularly sections (2) and (3), and the subsequent administrative regulations seemed to point out the divergent concepts about the cause(s) of poverty and the way in which it was to be eliminated. It can be argued that the differences in suggested action strategies derive from basically differing conceptions of the poor, or—more likely—of the problem of poverty. In contrast to an approach oriented to social service or rehabilitation, for example, the rhetoric surrounding the Community Action Program spoke of institutional changes and neighborhood-based political organizations created to offset the sense of powerlessness and lack of hope imputed to be found among low income people. The late Senator Robert Kennedy, in testimony before a House Committee, communicated some of the flavor of this position:

The institutions which affect the poor—education, welfare, recreation, business, labor—are huge, complex structures, operating far outside their control. They plan programs for the poor, not with them. Part of the sense of hopelessness and futility comes from the feeling of powerlessness to affect the operation of these organizations.

The community action programs must basically change these organizations by building into the program real representation of the poor. This bill calls for maximum feasible participation of the residents. This means the involvement of the poor in planning and implementing programs: giving them a real voice in their institutions.[12]

One basic change in the conceptualization of the problem by the Community Action Program was its departure from the moralistic stance implicit in the social deviance-as-individual-psychopathology perspective. In *The Politics of Poverty* John C. Donovan notes,

Only Title II (the Community Action Program) was strikingly new . . . community action was fervently anti-establishment; schools, employment services, welfare agencies, city hall, were all part of an "establishment" or "system" which served "the disadvantaged" by referring them from one "helping service" to another without ever really understanding or challenging the "culture of poverty" and with no real ability to move families out of poverty.[13]

The impetus for this conceptual development came from the President's Committee on Juvenile Delinquency: "As a criteria (sic) for the receipt of funds (from the President's Committee), communities were asked to indicate how they would plan for the attack on the problem, which was defined as *primarily rooted in the social structure,* rather than in personality failure." [14]

That such changes in the local community structure could be achieved seemed more a part of the liberals' optimism than an accurate forecast of future events. A staff member of the President's Committee noted in this regard, "A half century of local structure and tradition and style does not shift easily and without trauma." [15]

Reaction from the traditional structure, or at least from one of its foremost institutions—City Hall—was not long in coming. In its 1965 Report, the United States Conference of Mayors stated:

Whereas no responsible Mayor can accept the implication in the OEO Workbook that the goals of this program can only be achieved by creating tensions between the poor and the existing agencies and by fostering class struggle: NOW THEREFORE BE IT RE-SOLVED that the administration be urged to insure that any policy ... assure the continuing control of any expenditures relative to this program by the fiscally responsible local officials. [16]

The power behind the Mayors, according to Peter Marris and Martin Rein, is the traditional American value of local autonomy: "Even problems common to the whole society tend to be seen as a complex of local difficulties to which national policy should offer support rather than direction." [17] Three specific problems noted by "activist social scientists" associated with the President's Committee and the Task Force planning the Community Action Program were the fragmentation of available services, the lack of responsiveness from traditional community institutions to the needs of the poor, and the lack of involvement or participation by the poor in the planning and administering of programs.

Thus far, it is hoped that the reader has seen the potential for conflict among ideas, programs, and organizations that quickly dominated the national scene once poverty became an issue in the public domain, with resources available to communities to respond to the issue as they defined it. This study will examine the alternative views of the problem as they were manifest in the literature and will group the various perspectives into three ideal type explanations of poverty in America. Strategies for action will be related to causal explanations of the problem. Comparisons will then be made between the planned community action concept and the operationalized community action program. The purpose for this investigation will be to analyze the planning function as it was manifest in this effort to combat one of our nation's major problems. An underlying assumption of the author, perhaps better called a "value," is the need for coherence in social action or intervention aimed at the resolution of such problems. The need for coherence carries with it the prerequisites of explaining a problem, developing strategies for change consistent with the explanation, and assuming responsibility for their implementation. The Community Action Program of the Office of Economic Opportunity is the setting in which this exploration will be carried out.

THE THEORETICAL PERSPECTIVE OF THE STUDY

The decision to attack a major community problem such as poverty through the undefined administrative relationship between the federal government and the local community inevitably created a context of uncertainty at both levels. James Thompson notes that "organizations abhor uncertainty" [18] and act to reduce or eliminate it. It is of vital importance to under-

stand the measures taken to adapt to the concept of a new
organization on the local community scene, especially when
this new actor brings with it the opportunity to gain substantial sums of money and undefined guidelines for attracting it.
The response of the existing organizational field to this new
entity, the convergence of the local organizations with the
federal agency with regard to concepts of the problem and the
means to solve it, and the determinants of local program output
are issues which can be viewed from both a theoretical and
practical stance. We will turn now to the theoretical view.

In *The Community in America*,[19] Roland L. Warren discusses
the impact of "the great change" in American community life,
change precipitated by increased industrialization and urban-
ization as these phenomena have affected local autonomy. His
concept of the community as a network of local organizational
interaction ("the horizontal pattern") and simultaneously as
part of a broader network involving extra-community organizations ("the vertical pattern") at the state, regional, and
federal levels suggests that further description of the functioning of local community decision organizations [20] within both
arenas is in order. The Community Action Program, with
federal status as an agency in the Executive Office of the President and a mandate to operate its programs through a locally
created organization, the Community Action Agency, offers an
excellent opportunity to observe the relationships between
actors in both horizontal and vertical systems.

Warren's paper, "The Interorganizational Field as a Focus
for Investigation," describes the multiplicity of "community
decision organizations" in communities throughout the nation:
such organizations "purported to—and in varying degrees
(were) legitimated to—represent the interests of the community in some segment of broad community concern. . . . Such
organizations constitute the means through which the community attempts to concert certain decisions and activities."[21]
Each community decision organization (CDO) is seen as oper-

ating within its own more or less defined domain, but pursuing its own goals while interacting with other organizations in the horizontal system or local interorganizational field: "It has often been observed that communities as such do not have a single organizational structure, but rather are constituted of many formal structures (including that of the municipal government), as well as interaction patterns through which locality-relevant decisions, in one or another segment of community activities, are made." [22] The problem of concerted decision-making involving CDO's becomes an active concern in the uncertain situation in which a new CDO—here the Community Action Agency—is brought into the horizontal system. The issue becomes further intensified when this new organization is charged with comprehensive responsibility which cuts across previously negotiated agency boundaries and has access to funds from a new extra-community resource (in this case, the Office of Economic Opportunity).

At the crux of the problem for existing local organizations is their position in the horizontal system vis-a-vis the new organization in the community. In the perpetual competition between organizations for resources necessary to attainment of their goals, some organizations are able to influence the decisions of any new agency. These influential organizations are defined by Warren as the "input constituency." [23] The interrelationship of any local organization with its environment or interorganizational field is discussed at length in recent studies of organizational interaction. [24]

Selznick defines "constituency" ". . . (as) a group, formally outside a given organization, to which the latter (or an element within it) has a special commitment." [25] Warren further refines this definition to describe the "input constituency" as "consisting of those parties to which (the local community decision organization) acknowledges a responsibility in determining its policy and program." [26] This process is made more explicit in the case of the creation of a new organization within the horizontal system and the necessity for interaction between this new actor and the organizational environment or the horizontal system. Selznick emphasizes this point in an article directly relevant to the creation of a new local organization, "Critical Decisions in Organizational Development," in which he says "The early phase of an institution's life is marked by a scrutiny of its own capabilities and of its environment, to discover where its resources are and on whom it is dependent . . . and the future evolution of the institution is largely conditioned by the commitments generated in this basic decision." [27] One such basic decision regards the composition of the input constituency and its influence on eventual program output.

This concern with interaction around organizational goal-setting is continued in Thompson's book, *Organizations in Action*, where he develops the concept of organizational domain. He states that all viable organizations must establish a domain, "claims which an organization stakes out for itself in terms of (1) range of products, (2) population served, and (3) services rendered." [28] He goes on to suggest that the "organization's domain identifies the point at which the organization is dependent upon inputs from the environment. The composition of the environment, the location within it of capabilities, in turn determines upon whom the organization is dependent." [29] Implicit in these statements is the notion that somehow organizations within the same environment work out boundaries regarding preservation of various components of their domains—resources, clientele, service areas, etc. But it is far from clear how this process—either planned or negotiated—works itself out; nor is there adequate information about the conditions under which collaboration between organizations takes place. This problem becomes even more complex when the organizational interaction involves extra-community institutions and their influences upon local organizational interaction.

Norton Long describes the local community interorganizational network as an "ecology of games,"[30] a largely functional unstructured territorial system which is maintained by the players of the games going on in the community. He points out that this form of interaction, called by Scott Greer "a minimal ordering,"[31] "has been developed over time, and there are general expectations as to the interaction."[32] One source of potential interruption in this ongoing process is intervention in the "ecology" from extra-community sources of influence. Long postulates the response from the local territorial system: "The need or cramp in the system presents itself to the players of the game as an opportunity for them to exploit or a menace to be overcome."[33] These alternative possibilities can be explored through the example of a new organization being developed within the local community, given the prerequisite interaction with the environment and the required establishment of an organizational domain for the new actor. The fact that the new organization brings with it guidelines developed outside the local community poses the issue of how the horizontal system with its minimal ordering and established rules of the game will "manage" the imposed regulations and related domain matters. Should there be some inconsistency between the existing players of the games and the new actor as to general expectations regarding the division of the domain, further problems can be predicted. The entire procedure of negotiation which ensues from the local-federal relationship explicit in the insertion into the local community of a new organization financed by federal funds raises questions about local autonomy. We have seen that these questions were posed by Warren, who asserted that the demise of local autonomy would accompany "the great change." It will remain the task of this study to examine this issue; this will be done at a later point when the data covering program output is presented and analyzed.

It is clear that questions remain regarding the process of

organizational interaction within the local community and that these questions become more pointed when aspects of the vertical system are involved. The complexities of rational social planning involving organizational interaction at the community level and between the local level and federal level emerged in the development of the Community Action Program. When the added dimensions of innovation in programming and a structural change strategy are folded in, the process of constructing a problem definition and action strategy provide the opportunity to examine organizational behavior and the enactment of social legislation.

Of implied significance is the degree to which planned social change—in fact, social planning itself—can occur. The literature on this issue ranges from advocacy of change as largely unplanned, to change as largely within some planned framework. Between these two ends on the continuum are ranged several positions on the plausibility of inclusive or concerted planning at the community level called by their various proponents "incremental planning," "adaptive planning," or "opportunistic decision-making." In order to discuss the interaction of the local community action agency with the horizontal system, or the interaction of the local and federal systems, we must examine the potential and actual operation of social planning as it relates to these interactions.

The availability of new federal funds to establish a local attack on poverty created an action system within the local interorganizational field around the necessity to respond to this opportunity, whether challenge or threat. The administrative guidelines for the new local community action agency required the coordination of local resources without specifying the priority of operational goals or the form the new organization was to take. The *CAP Guide, Instructions to Applicants* emphasizes, "The most effective and desirable community action program is one which is broad-based, organized on a community-wide basis, and involves the coordination of a variety of anti-poverty actions. A broadly-based, coordinated program should embrace components in all of the major service systems. . . ."[34] The questions raised by the absence of specific action or detailed regulations inevitably created uncertainty about the domains of existing organizations and also may have threatened the boundary system between these organizations. With the responsibility for the creation of the new agency being a predominantly local matter, and the participation of the traditional agencies not clearly delineated, the arena and/ or domain to be worked out for the new CAA was vague and uncertain.

This study will look at the outcome of this uncertainty, concentrating on the influence exerted by the existing horizontal system, as it became part of the new organization's input constituency and made what Selznick described as the originating vital decisions regarding the local CAA domain. The role of the early actors in this developmental stage of the CAA, those people comprising what Sower et al. call the "initiation set,"[35] will be examined in relation to the program output of the CAA.

The multiple problems encountered by the CAA in communities across the country will then be analyzed. The analytic perspective will involve issues of the explanation of poverty, the relationship of action strategy to the explanation of the problem, program planning, and organizational interaction. The methodology used and the procedures followed will be discussed in Chapter 2. Chapters 3–5 will explore three differing conceptualizations of the problem of poverty and the derived action strategies related to each. The development of the Community Action Program will be analyzed in Chapter 6. Chapter 7 will then present and examine the data collected from the community action agencies in twenty cities, comparing operational outcomes with planned outcomes. Finally, Chapters 8 and 9 will discuss the findings of the study, and point out the author's sense of their implications.

NOTES

[1] Johnson, Lyndon B., quoted in *Poverty in Affluence*, Robert E. Will and Harold G. Vatter, eds. (New York: Harcourt, Brace & World, Inc., 1965), p. 16.

[2] Coser, Lewis A., "The Sociology of Poverty," in *Social Problems*, Vol. 13 No. 2 (Fall, 1965), p. 141.

[3] *Ibid*, p. 143.

[4] *Ibid*, p. 143.

[5] Goldwater, Barry, *New York Times*, July 19, 1961.

[6] Goldwater, Barry, *New York Times*, January 16, 1964.

[7] Galbraith, John K., *The Affluent Society* (Boston: Houghton Mifflin Company, 1958), p. 325.

[8] Lumer, Hyman, *Poverty: Its Roots and Its Future* (New York: International Publishers Company, Inc., 1965), p. 22.

[9] Moynihan, Daniel P., *Maximum Feasible Misunderstanding* (New York: Arkville Press, 1969).

[10] Wofford, John G., "The Politics of Local Responsibility — Administration of the Community Action Program, 1964–1966," in James L. Sundquist, ed., *On Fighting Poverty* (New York: Basic Books, Inc., 1969), p. 1.

[11] Economic Opportunity Act of 1964, 78 Stat. 508 (1964).

[12] Donovan, John C., *The Politics of Poverty* (New York: Western Publishing Company, 1967), p. 35.

[13] *Ibid*, pp. 38–41.

[14] Kravitz, Sanford L., "Community Action Programs: Past, Present, Future," *American Child*, Vol. 47 No. 4 (November 1965), p. 2.

[15] *Ibid*, p. 31.

[16] United States Conference of Mayors, 1965 Report.

[17] Marris, Peter, and Rein, Martin, *The Dilemmas of Social Reform* (New York: Atherton Press, 1967), pp. 8–9.

[18] Thompson, James D., *Organizations in Action* (New York: McGraw-Hill, 1967).

[19] Warren, Roland L., *The Community In America* (Chicago: Rand McNally & Company, 1963).

[20] The term "Community Decision Organizations" comes from: Warren, Roland L., "The Interaction of Community Decision Organizations," *Social Service Review*, Vol. 41 No. 3 (September 1967) .

[21] Warren, Roland L., "The Interorganizational Field as a Focus for Investigation," *Administrative Science Quarterly*, Vol. 12 No. 3, (December 1967), p. 400.

[22] *Ibid*, p. 401.

[23] *Ibid*, p. 401.

[24] Warren, Roland, L., *op. cit.;* Thompson, James D., and McEwan, William J., "Organizational Goals and Environment: Goal Setting as an Interaction Process," *American Sociological Review*, 23 (February 1958); Dill, William R., "The Impact of Environment on Organizational Development," in *Concepts and Issues in Administrative Behavior*, Sidney Mailick and Edward H. Van Ness, eds., (Englewood Cliffs: Prentice-Hall, 1962); Thompson, James D., *op. cit.;* Emery, S. E., and Trist, E. L., "The Causal

Texture of Organizational Environments," *Human Relations,* 18 (February 1965); Evan, William M., "The Organization-Set: Toward a Theory of Interorganizational Relations," in James D. Thompson, ed., *Approaches to Organizational Design* (Pittsburgh: University of Pittsburgh Press (1966).

25 Selznick, Philip, *TVA and the Grass Roots: A Study in the Sociology of Formal Organization* (Berkeley: University of California Press, 1953), p. 145.

26 Warren, Roland L., "Interorganizational Field," *op. cit.* p. 409.

27 Selznick, Philip, "Critical Decisions in Organizational Development," in *Complex Organizations,* Amitai Etzioni, ed., (New York: Holt, Rinehart & Winston, 1964), p. 356.

28 Thompson, *Organizations in Action,* p. 26.

29 *Ibid,* pp. 26–27.

30 Long, Norton, "The Local Community as an Ecology of Games," in *The Polity,* (Chicago: Rand McNally & Company, 1962).

31 Greer, Scott, *The Emerging City: Myth and Reality,* (Glencoe: The Free Press, 1962), p. 200.

32 Long, "The Local Community as an Ecology of Games," p. 143.

33 *Ibid.,* p. 144.

34 *Community Action Program Guide,* Vol. 1 (February 1965), pp. 16–17.

35 Sower, Christopher, et al., *Community Involvement* (Glencoe: The Free Press, 1957).

CHAPTER II

The Construction of Ideal Types and Method of Procedure

CONSTRUCTION OF IDEAL TYPES

A REVIEW of the literature on poverty and the poor led the author to attempt the development of a typology or classification of the many varying and often contradictory description-conceptualizations of the problem. Using causal explanation (which at times is explicit in the arguments made and at other times is derived from the discussion) as a criterion variable, three ideal types—or categories of description-explanations, or definitions—of the problem of poverty were developed for heuristic purposes; that is, for aggregating independently conceived means of conceptualizing poverty. The use of ideal types as a heuristic device is not uncommon. The usefulness of ideal types is based on the work of Max Weber,[1] while the application of this procedure to understanding poverty has been explored by Charles Valentine.[2] Gerth and Mills, in writing about Weber, describe the concept:

The much discussed "ideal-type," a key term in Weber's methodological discussion, refers to the construction of certain elements of reality into a logically precise conception. The term "ideal" has nothing to do with evaluations of any sort. For analytical purposes, one may construct ideal types of prostitution as well as of religious leaders. The term does not mean that either harlots or prophets are exemplary or should be imitated as representatives of an ideal way of life. By using this term, Weber did not mean to introduce a new conceptual tool. He merely intended to bring a full awareness to what social scientists and historians had been doing when they used words like "the economic man," "feudalism," "Gothic versus Roman-esque architecture," or "kingship." He felt that social scientists had the choice of using logically controlled and unambiguous concep-tions, which are thus more removed from historical reality, or of using less precise concepts, which are more closely geared to the empirical world. Weber's interest in world-wide comparisons led him to consider extreme and "pure cases." These cases became "crucial instances" and controlled the level of abstraction that he used in connection with any particular problem. . . .

. . . As general concepts, ideal types are tools with which Weber prepares the descriptive materials of world history for comparative analysis. . . . His concern with specific historical problems and his interest in a comparative sociology of a generalizing nature are thus related; the difference between them is one of emphasis.[3]

In the process of creating an ideal type, several variables or attributes are combined from the work of numerous social scientists into a composite or whole. In this procedure the concepts developed by individual social scientists and selected for inclusion become subordinate to the more abstract level of the ideal type. The concepts thus become more removed from the description of the empirical phenomena for which they were originally created or utilized. Weber, in considering this process, notes:

This conceptual pattern brings together certain relationships and events of historical life into a complex, which is conceived as an internally consistent system. Substantively, this construct in itself is like a utopia which has been arrived at by the analytical accentua-tion of certain elements of reality. Its relationship to the empirical data consists solely in the fact that where market-conditioned rela-tionships of the type referred to by the abstract construct are discov-ered or suspected to exist in reality to some extent, we can make the characteristic features of this relationship pragmatically clear and understandable by reference to an ideal type. . . . It is not a descrip-tion of reality but it aims to give unambiguous means of expression to such a description. . . . An ideal type is formed by the one-sided accentuation of one or more points of view and by the synthesis of a great many diffuse, discrete, more or less present and occasionally absent concrete individual phenomena, which are arranged according to those one-sided emphasized viewpoints into a unified analytical construct (Gedankenbild). In its conceptual purity, this mental construct (Gedankenbild) cannot be found empirically anywhere in reality.[4]

In this study, a multitude of varying concepts of poverty will be classified according to three constructed ideal types of explanation of the causes of poverty.

In order to understand the relationship between the definition of the problem, social action strategies, and related organizational interaction, the author has found it both necessary and useful to construct these ideal type categories. This process is a step required for examining the progression from explanation of the problem to planned intervention strategy to implementation of programs, whether the issue addressed be poverty, disease, or any other societal problem.

The three ideal type categories of explanation of the existence of poverty in an otherwise affluent America are labeled "The Culture of Poverty," "The Dysfunctional Social System," and "The Dysfunctional Economic System." The categories or ideal types are composed of the following five dimensions:

1) The conception of poverty as an independent or dependent variable.
2) The participation of the poor in the broader American culture, i.e., the existence of a subculture of the poor.
3) The existence of a "poverty cycle" or a "tangle of pathology."
4) The relationship of the poor to the non-poor within American society.
5) Methods for the elimination of poverty.

An outline of the three ideal types and of the variations between them on the five specified dimensions will follow a brief discussion of each variable.

Whether poverty is defined as caused by deviant behavior

or whether deviant behavior is perceived as caused by poverty is a controversy argued by both social scientists and politicians. At least two distinct conceptualizations of this issue have emerged which contradict one another; in almost all cases some discussion advocating one or the other of these views emerges. At one extreme is the position that the poor are poor because they not only behave in a fashion unacceptable to the norms of society; they also have a distinctly different value system which condones such deviant behavior. At the other extreme is the argument that while statistics on deviant behavior include disproportionately high percentages of poor people, the behavior depicted is an existential reaction to the debasement and frustration of living in the condition of poverty caused by an unjust and dysfunctional social system.

Whether a distinct "subculture" of the poor exists or does not exist also stands as a controversial point among social scientists. To a degree, one's position on this point relates to the definition he uses of both "culture" and "subculture." As Valentine points out, it has become fashionable to attach the term "culture" to many social subgroups[5]; examples of such intellectual fadism include "slum culture," "youth culture," etc. Part of this act of attribution involves the assertion that the values of the subgroup support the behavior of its members. The assumed compatability between behavior and values suggests to some social scientists that a third factor, preferred goals, is included in the description of low income life styles. It is this assumption of preference which leads to discussion of the poverty subgroup as a culturally or subculturally distinct entity. In contrast, Valentine points out,

Our growing understanding of the part played by values in cultural systems has thus helped to expose one of the crudities of conventional wisdom. This is the simple misconception that people everywhere live as they do because they prefer their actual mode of existence and its consequences. Indeed, there can be few human situations that allow full enactment of cultural values in the practical

world. So we have come to suspect that either romantic ennoble-
ment or unwarranted debasement of the subject is at work when a
people's values are simply inferred directly from the surface aspects
of their lives.[6]

Thus, the battle rages between those who advocate one or
another of these positions. This dimension, however, should
be flagged by the reader, for its importance in decisions of
social policy will be considered at length at a later point.

  The existence of poverty through several generations of the
same family or the complex of poverty-related problems resid-
ing in an individual poor family presents another disputed
issue. The controversy over this issue is evidenced by several
varying positions in the literature. On occasion each perception
includes quantitative data in support of its position. Perhaps
the most acrimonious debate on this issue focuses on "The
Moynihan Report" or "The Negro Family: The Case for National Action."[7] Advocates of Moynihan's position argue that
pathology and deviance are so pervasive that people are prevented from exploiting those opportunities which are available
to them. Moynihan's critics argue from a perspective that
Herbert Gans has called the "situational view of social change;
they suggest that people will respond to the situations—and
opportunities—available to them, and change their behavior
accordingly."[8] Still another view contends that continual existence in poverty inhibits an individual's capacity to learn the
skills prerequisite to entering the labor force. Thus, as with
the other dimensions discussed above, this one also shows
divergent points of view, contradictory values and competing
contentions.

  Another area of concern, more often implicit in the literature
than directly discussed, relates to what might be called variations in life styles. This dimension, focused on the relationship
between the poor and the non-poor, is not without its share of
opposing perspectives. The basic issue seems to be one of "ap-

propriate" or normative life patterns or behaviors; on the one
hand, the argument is made that the poor form a distinct group
who have little in common with "mainstream" American life,
who do not participate in its culture or social milieu. In contrast, it is contended that the poor play a distinct role in American life, share in the culture, but are denied access to the
resources necessary to affect mainstream behavioral and taste
patterns. At this latter pole, the point is occasionally argued
that to hold the subcultural perspective is equivalent to cultural imperialism; it assumes the inferiority of behavior patterns which differ from the mainstream. At the core of this
dilemma is the basic question: Are the poor really different
from the non-poor in what they want for themselves, in what
they value highly, or in their aspirations?

The reader may have seen that each of the first four dimensions contains within it implications for social policies regarding the elimination of poverty. The differences in viewpoint
on this matter range as wide as those that have preceded it.
The criterion variable in examining various proposals for the
elimination of poverty is the emphasis on who or what is to be
changed: On one side, there are various strategies for changing the individual in some way, whether it be his manners,
his skill level, his values, or his behavior; on the other hand,
there are methods for changing either the social or economic
structure of the society. When competition for funds necessary
to administer the poverty war became a part of the American
scene, the competition between policy recommendations became more real and was fought out at both the local and
national levels.

Thus, we have five dimensions to the ideal type categories.
It might be added that the construction of the ideal types was
an inductive process, of reading and piecing together a multitude of books, articles and monographs, in the attempt to grasp
coherently the facets of the intellectual conflicts which par-

alleled the strategy and organizational battles fought in the war on poverty. Below are outlines of the ideal types as they integrate each of the five dimensions discussed above.

Three Ideal Type Conceptualizations of Poverty

I. *The Culture of Poverty*
A. The lower class possesses a distinct subculture manifest in deviant behaviors, values and focal concerns (not present in the dominant culture); this subculture determines their socio-economic position.

B. The major difference between the culture of poverty and the broader American culture is that the normative behavior patterns and values of the poverty culture are deviant from those of the broader culture.

C. The poverty subculture constitutes a self-generating cycle, transmitted to children at an early age, and perpetuated both by the pattern of socialization to deviant values and behaviors and by the consequent psycho-social inadequacies which prohibit escape.

D. The poverty subculture must be eliminated, and the poor assimilated to middle class or working class value patterns before poverty itself can be done away with.

E. In contemporary American society, the elimination of poverty can be accomplished through directed culture change, social work, psychiatric therapies and compensatory education.

II. *The Dysfunctional Social System*
A. The lower class forms a distinct subsociety manifest in deprived socio-economic circumstances; these result from a dysfunctional social structure.

B. The distinctive behavior patterns occurring among the poor are normal adaptions to the frustration which comes from adherence to the cultural goals and values of a broader society, cultural goals which the social structure prevents the poor from attaining.

C. The structural position and subsocietal behavior patterns of the poor stem from historical and contemporary situations which generally involve lack of access to the political and economic systems, systematic racial discrimination, ineffective social institutions, and other factors which also prohibit rather than facilitate full participation in the larger society.

D. In order for poverty to be eliminated, two changes have to be brought about simultaneously: alterations of the social structure to guarantee the poor equal access to economic opportunity and increased power for the poor vis-a-vis the institutions which affect their lives.

E. In contemporary American society, the most likely source for the changes necessary to eliminate poverty is the organization of the poor to enable them to exercise political power, to participate in the planning and administration of relevant programs, and to increase their control over the institutions instrumental in their lives.

III. *The Dysfunctional Economic System*

A. The existence of a lower economic class is the result of structural unemployment, inadequate income maintenance programs, and low levels of productivity.

B. The lower class is made up of distinct subgroups in America which can be characterized by their relative isolation from the dynamics of the national economy.

C. Those groups existing in relative isolation from general economic growth will remain poor because of inadequate income maintenance programs.

D. In order for poverty to be eliminated, adequate income maintenance programs must be created as a first step; they must be supplemented by economic policies aimed at expansion of the economy and its attendant benefits.

E. Changes in income maintenance policies at the national level are necessary to eliminate poverty. They must focus on continued stimulation of the economy to promote increased employment. Local derivatives of this approach will be oriented around income-producing programs.

METHOD OF PROCEDURE IN THIS STUDY

The next step in this study will be to determine—implicitly or explicitly, where possible—the social action or program strategies that exist within each ideal type definition of poverty. Conceptually, this process postulates that, for a given alternative means of explaining the existence of poverty, there will be a given alternative means of perceiving the solution, which will be internally consistent with the ideal type. Thus, parallel to the ideal type concepts of the problem, three distinct action or program strategies will emerge, each related to one of the ideal types. The relationship between the ideal type and the derived program strategy appears below:

Ideal Type	*Program Strategy*
The Culture of Poverty	Individual and Cultural Change
The Dysfunctional Social System	Institutional Change
The Dysfunctional Economic System	Change in Economic Policies

The strategy of Individual and Cultural Change is focused on altering the individual's "deviant" behavior, his perceived individual defects (ego weakness, for example) and his inadequate exposure to the dominant culture. Operationally, this type of strategy is manifest in such programs as remedial education, cultural enrichment, all forms of psychiatric and social work therapies, family life education, and vocational counseling that is not directly linked to a specific job. Martin Rein examines the policy implications of such an approach, commenting: "What is at issue is the (individual's) capacity to use institutions, rather than the relevance of the functions which these institutions carry out."[9] The derivation of this strategy from the Culture of Poverty ideal type will be discussed at length in Chapter 3.

The strategy related to The Dysfunctional Social System ideal type, or Institutional Change, focuses on altering the present relationship between institutions and the low income utilizers of their services. The basic approach requires increasing the power and influence of the poor vis-a-vis the service agencies through enabling the poor to participate in the planning and administration of programs, through opening the institutional structure by creating new types of employment roles (as opposed to new job openings in traditional areas of employment), through developing new local organizations of poor people to compete with and pressure the traditional agencies, and through increasing the amount of local resources committed to programs aimed at the elimination of poverty. Operationally, the Institutional Change Strategy includes such efforts as community or neighborhood organization programs, voter registration campaigns, job development or New Careers projects, and advocacy planning experiments. This approach assumes that existing societal institutions function in a manner which condones the existence of poverty and serve to maintain their own organizational interests and position in the existing social order.

The strategy for the third ideal type, The Dysfunctional Economic System, is Change in Economic Policies. This strategy has both national and local foci. On the national level, the operational programs include a full employment policy, increased minimum wage coverage, increased social security coverage, creation of a guaranteed annual income plan, and alternative means of stimulating the national economy toward an even greater gross national product. On the local level, programmatic manifestations of this strategy would include income-producing projects such as on-the-job-training, and other manpower programs which emphasize increasing workers' skills while providing for guaranteed employment.

After we have constructed more fully the three ideal type conceptualizations of poverty and their respective strategies for its elimination, we will review and analyze materials prepared by the Task Force on Urban Areas (the architects of the Community Action Program) and the speeches or papers given by individual members of the Task Force. The definition of the Task Force's concept of poverty will then be compared to the three ideal types and a classification made of their orientation both on the conceptual and operational continuums.

Having established the intellectual bases of the planned Community Action Program and its intended outcome, the study will proceed to examine program data from the local community action agencies in twenty cities across the nation. The program data, conceived of as the output of the local community action agencies, was collected as part of a study of citizen participation in community action.

Program data, giving the title of each individually developed program or "component" within each city, was analyzed in terms of the operational definitions developed to describe the three social action strategies derived from the ideal types. Each of the 350 components funded in the twenty cities will be classified according to one of the three social action strategies. The total program outputs for the twenty cities will then be classified in accordance with the ideal type explanation of the problem to which they were addressed and its related strategy for remedying or eliminating that problem. Comparisons with the anticipated outcome inferred from the national CAP planners' position as stipulated in the Task Force will then be made. In addition, data regarding the constituencies of the initiators and developers of the twenty local programs will also be examined to determine the extent to which each community acted upon the mandate for "maximum feasible participation of residents of the areas and members of the groups served." Comparison of the local community action agency program output with the inferred interests of the local group of initiators and developers will be made and speculations as to alternative definitions of the problem offered to

account for any divergence between planned and actual outcome. At this point, it is sufficient to note the expectation that
a substantial number of programs in each city differed in both
the definition of the problem and social action strategy from
what could be projected from the Task Force's position.

To the extent that there is a difference between the concepts
of the national planners and the products of the local administrators, what factors account for the disjunction? Certainly
one phenomenon under examination will be the national
planners' attempt to legislate reform at the local level. Implicit
in this analysis will be consideration of the plausibility of
planned institutional change and its assumed capacity for centrally planned reform. The assumptions made about the local
community action system, or the local "interorganizational
field," by the planner-reformers of the Task Force will be examined. We will also explore their commitment to three salient
concepts which formed the substantive development of their
plans: coordination (or comprehensive programming), innovation, and citizen participation. Further, given the Task Force's
insistence on the creation of a *local* community action agency,
the planners' failure to account for its maintenance needs and
day-to-day operational practices in terms of formal organizational theory will be pursued.

In order to examine these issues, four processes will be
undertaken:

1) A review of the administrative regulations imposed by
   the national Office of Economic Opportunity-Commu-
   nity Action Program will be conducted. It is suggested
   that several of these regulations, particularly those
   focused on cooperation and coordination among local
   service systems, may contain within them the bases of
   the contradictions of the stated goals of the program.

2) An analysis of the entrance of a new organization (with
   newly available funds from the extra-community or ver-

tical system) into the local community interorganizational network will be undertaken. The response from
the local community or horizontal system will be observed: Which community decision organizations were
involved in creating the CAA? How were the traditional
agencies involved, if at all? How was the structure of
the new agency developed? And with what results?

3) An examination will be conducted of the critical influence
that early organizational actors have in determining later
outcomes. What role did the early organizational actors
play in determining the CAA output, as measured by
the program strategy pursued? Did organizations investing time or other resources in developing the CAA get
a return on their investment?

4) A questioning of the potential for planned social structural change will begin with the study of the Task Force
planners' Social Systemic view of the causes of the problem, and its related institutional change strategy. Can a
local CAA—composed as it is of various segments of the
horizontal system—be expected to bring about institutional change in that system?

Each of the four sections above will raise important questions. Analysis of the program outcome in each of the twenty
cities, and obviously across the cities, will indicate that the
planned format and strategy of the national Community Action
Program planners was not followed. It will be posited that the
reason for this divergence was that their basic view of the
problem was not acceptable in local communities. In addition,
questions will be raised about the feasibility of the Task Force
strategy and its plan for implementation. The answers to these
questions will be sought from examination of the data. We
will also examine the data in an effort to substantiate several
more general hypotheses relating the involvement of organizations from the horizontal system to various aspects of the
CAA. These hypotheses are:

1) The greater the involvement of organizations from the horizontal system (as measured by either their representation in the group of initiators and developers of the local CAA or by their ability to capture programs funded by the local CAA on a contractual basis, or both of these), the lower the level of program administration by the community action agency.

2) The greater the involvement of organizations from the horizontal system, the greater the efficiency of the CAA in attracting funds from the Office of Economic Opportunity (as measured by per capita funds attracted).

3) The greater the involvement of organizations from the horizontal system, the greater the likelihood of the Individual or Cultural Change strategy, the less the likelihood of the Institutional Change or the Income-Producing strategies.

NOTES

[1] Weber, Max, *The Methodology of the Social Sciences,* Edward A. Shils and Henry A. Finch, eds. (Glencoe: The Free Press, 1949).

[2] Valentine, Charles, *Culture and Poverty* (Chicago: University of Chicago Press, 1968).

[3] Gerth, H. H. and Mills, C. Wright, *From Max Weber: Essays in Sociology,* (New York: Oxford University Press, 1958), pp. 59–60.

[4] Weber, *The Methodology of the Social Sciences,* p. 15.

[5] Valentine, *Culture and Poverty,* p. 15.

[6] *Ibid,* pp. 7–8.

[7] *The Negro Family: The Case for National Action,* U.S. Department of Labor, Washington, D.C., 1965.

[8] Gans, Herbert J., "Poverty and Culture: Some Basic Questions about Methods of Studying Life-Styles of the Poor," paper presented at the International Seminar on Poverty, Essex University, April 1967, p. 6.

[9] Rein, Martin, "Social Science and the Elimination of Poverty," in *Journal of the American Institute of Planners,* Vol. XXXIII No. 3 (May 1967), p. 151.

CHAPTER III

The Culture of Poverty

Two salient and interrelated concepts are pertinent to the establishment of the culture of poverty ideal type: pathology and deviance. Both concepts describe behavior which does not conform to middle class standards. The word pathology suggests that the behavior involved is non-voluntary, similar to an illness. Those afflicted by pathology, whose "illness" is not part of their intended behavior, are portrayed as victims of forces beyond their control. Deviance, on the other hand, is defined as willed violation of existing norms and values. Both pathology and deviance are seen as pervasive in the lower class. The saturation of these behaviors in the lower classes, often supported by a deviant value system, invariably leads the children of the poor into non-conforming life patterns. The culture of poverty theorists acknowledge and legitimize the existing societal norms and values while implying disapproval of those who are described as deviating from them. Where the deviation is on the individual level, it is labeled pathology. Various diagnostic categories exist within psychiatric terminology to describe differences in abnormal behavior and much research exists to document the case that more of this type of behavior is found in the lower socio-economic class than in the other strata of American society. When aggregates of individuals are perceived to be significantly different or non-conforming, they are frequently said to constitute a subculture. One such subculture has popularly become known as the culture of poverty.

The easy transition from being individually pathological in

terms of the broader society's conception of appropriate behavior to being a deviant member of a subcultural group can
be traced by examining some of the alleged abnormal characteristics of the individual poor person and following how
these characteristics are considered to be naturally acquired
from his defective environment. A brief historical note is in
order here, reminding the reader of the clear distinction made
throughout the history of this country between the deserving
and the undeserving poor, between the poor and the pauper.
This distinction parallels perceived differences between the
pathological and the deviant poor. The differences between
the two categories were well expressed shortly after the turn
of the century by Robert Hunter:

Paupers are not, as a rule, unhappy. They are not ashamed; they are
not keen to become independent; they are not bitter or discontented.
They have passed over the line which separates poverty from pauperism. . . . This distinction between the poor and paupers may be
seen everywhere. They are in all large cities in America and abroad,
streets and corners and alleys where a class of people live who have
lost all self-respect and ambition, who rarely, if ever, work, who are
aimless and drifting, who like drink, who have no thought for their
children, and who live more or less contentedly on rubbish and alms.
Such districts are . . . in all cities everywhere. The lowest level of
humanity is reached in these districts . . . This is pauperism. There
is no mental agony here; they do not work sore; there is no dread;
they live miserably, but they do not care.[1]

This strong statement attributes several characteristics to
the poor which form recurrent themes in the literature aggre-
grated into the culture of poverty ideal type. Among those
behavioral traits which receive almost uniform treatment are
the lack of ambition, refusal to work, apathy, and neglect in
child care. Of even greater importance, in terms of the concept of a subculture or a culture of poverty, is the belief that
such behaviors are supported or condoned by a system of
values which differ markedly from those of the working class

or middle class. Hunter notes that the group he classifies as
paupers is not generally "unhappy;" they live more or less contentedly and they suffer little mental agony. The criterion
variable determining membership in a distinct subculture or,
more specifically for our purposes, in the culture of poverty
seems to be the existence of a deviant value system which
supports the behaviors specified as deviant.

The single dimension receiving the greatest attention is the
relation of the pauper to the work force. Here the advocates
of the culture of poverty perspective define the lack of participation in the work force by the poverty-stricken as a voun-
tary and therefore deviant act. Hunter pointed this out, and
others supported him:

Work was regarded as virtueless — a necessary evil to be avoided
when necessary.[2]

The disreputable poor are the people who remain unemployed or
casually or irregularly employed, even during periods approaching
full employment and prosperity . . .[3]

The best possible thing for a worker is to work. He is more satisfied
and he is happier, but he does not understand this.[4]

Authors of this persuasion note that a component of the
lower class poor person's view of work is a deficient level of
aspiration and ambition. While certain authors take limited
opportunties into account, the culture of poverty perspective
includes an aspect of voluntary lack of success in work: "To
put it simply the lower class individual doesn't want as much
success, knows he couldn't get it even if he wanted to, and
doesn't want what might help him get success."[5] Consistent
with this position is the idea that achievement is a combination
of ability and motivation, with the lower class perceived as
deficient in the latter. Numerous studies have been advanced
in support of this thesis, including those by Havinghurst and
Rodgers who document the lower levels of emphasis on college

education among the lower classes,[6] by Hyman, who comments, "A variety of data suggest that the lower class individual holds values of such a nature as to reduce his striving towards those ends which would result in his moving up the class structure;"[7] and by Centers and Cantril, who note the lower levels of desired occupations registered by lower class youth.[8]

In examining individuals and families from the lower classes, culture of poverty advocates find that pathological symptoms and various deviations frequently occur within the same individual or family. Two concepts describing the convergence of deviant behaviors and/or pathological symptoms deserve further attention: the "multiproblem family" and the "tangle of pathology." The multi-problem family has been the subject of study of several clinical investigators and social scientists interested in the provision of services to those in need. The State Communities Aid Association of New York surveyed literature on the multi-problem family prior to developing a research program related to this phenomenon. They found the best-known report to be from the Family-Centered Project of St. Paul, Minnesota, which said that

6% of the city's families accounted for 77% of its public assistance, 51% of its health services, and 56% of its adjustment services — in mental health, correction and casework. Similar findings were reported from studies in San Mateo County, California, Washington County, Maryland, and Winona County, Minnesota. Most dramatic of all, perhaps, was the finding of New York City's Youth Board that one (1) percent of families were responsible for 75% of the city's delinquency.[9]

Among the problems considered by the New York City Youth Board in their sample of multi-problem families were the following: poor school or social adjustment, mental illness or deficiency, chronic truancy, involvement of children in criminal acts, parents with physical illness, parental alcoholism and/or drug addiction, parental desertion, abuse and neglect of children, and illegitimacy.[10] Other definitions of the multi-problem family include:

A multi-problem family is one with a number of problems. In getting help for these problems, continuing service from a number of different welfare agencies is usually required. Most of these families would require public assistance . . . In spite of the many problems these families have and the number of agencies serving them, it is very difficult to reach these families in terms of tackling their basic problems. It has been found that if these families are helped with the current emergency which requires food, clothing, housing or medical care, they do not seek nor are they usually given help for the causes of their getting into the difficulty.[11]

The "hard core family," "multiple problem family," "hard-to-reach multi-problem family" — all these terms with implied definitions in combinations are used to describe those families which, in any community, are a grave concern to social workers and the community. While there may be no consensus in regard to definition, no one denies the existence of these families. It is generally agreed that these families seek help only at points of crisis to meet immediate needs, and do not accept and use constructively sustained planned help.[12]

A multi-problem family (is) one in which significant problems exist which the family either by itself or with help (has) not been able to resolve; such maladjustments create an intensive impact upon the family intrarelationships and the family interrelationships with the community.[13]

Definition of hard-to-reach, multi-problem family: Family in which parents and/or children have many serious problems of mind or body; who are (or are apt to become) a menace and/or a financial burden to the community because they appear to be unable to solve their problems themselves, or to seek to use constructively the community's resources for rehabilitative help.[14]

In general, the multi-problem family can be described as having more than its share of physical and emotional problems, a long history of financial dependency, poor housing, a frequently changing family unit, heavy incidence of mental illness and retardation, and a pattern of behavior that is often violent and in conflict with accepted social standards.[15]

The State Charities Aid Association of New York, in reviewing the literature about multi-problem families, developed a set of four criteria for this categorization:

1. Multiplicity of problems
2. Chrinocity of need
3. Resistance to treatment
4. Handicapping attitudes [16]

While the first three characteristics seem to describe adequately the pathological traits of the individual and of the family which spawned him, it is the last characteristic— "Handicapping attitudes"—which distinguishes the multi-problem or hard-to-reach family from other troubled family units. This feature is described by the research staff of the State Charities Aid Association:

Particularly among people of low socio-economic status, a combination of any or all of the following attitudes may constitute a handicap to the family in making its way in American community living: Hostility toward the school and hope that the children will drop out and "go to work," lack of "middle class drive" to get ahead, fear and suspicion of social workers and social agencies, hostility toward and fear of the police and law-enforcing authorities, the feeling that everybody (truant officer, children's court, bill collectors, teachers, social workers) is trying to "pick on people like us," lack of respect for one's or other's property, evaluation of uncouth language and sexual aggressiveness as desirable masculine traits, lack of appreciation for values of good health and preventive hygiene.[17]

It is the convergence of multiple problems with handcapping attitudes which Moynihan called the "tangle of pathology" and attributed to lower class black families. The tangle of pathology which concerned Moynihan had negative effects beyond their impact on those directly afflicted:

. . . because of housing segregation it is immensely difficult for the stable half to escape from the cultural influences of the unstable one. The children of middle-class Negroes often as not must grow up in, or next to the slums . . . They are therefore constantly exposed to the pathology of the disturbed group and constantly in danger of being drawn into it . . . In a word, most Negro youth are in danger of being caught up in the tangle of pathology that affects their world . . .[18]

Moynihan furthers the point previously suggested by those concerned about the multi-problem family. Poverty is an intergenerational problem; the children of the poor are most likely to succumb to the life style of their parents. This phenomenon is suggested by the Council of Economic Advisers in their 1964 *Economic Report of the President:*

Poverty breeds poverty. A poor individual or family has a high possibility of staying poor. Low incomes carry with them high risks of illness; limitations on mobility; limited access to education, information and training. Poor parents cannot give their children the opportunities for better health and education needed to improve their lot. Lack of motivation, hope and incentive is a more subtle but no less powerful barrier than lack of financial means. Thus the cruel legacy of poverty is passed from parents to children.[19]

Thus far, the culture of poverty ideal type has been portrayed as an attempt to explain high levels of individual psychopathology among the lower class, the convergence of more than one form of deviant behavior within the same lower class family (the multi-problem family), and especially the existence of highly deviant attitudes, beliefs, and values among the lower class which support or condone the overt behaviors existent among that stratum.

The method of accounting for the existence of a deviant value system is implicit in the use of the word "culture" in the phrase "the culture of poverty." Walter B. Miller, as an advocate of the "cultural approach" distinguishes it as a method which attempts to "understand the nature of cultural forces impinging upon the acting individual as they are perceived by the actor himself . . . rather than as they are perceived and evaluated from the reference position of another cultural system."[20] This style of investigation begins with customary behaviors as manifestations of "those patterned ways of acting, perceiving, and relating to one another which individuals share by virtue of the fact that they belong to a designated social grouping."[21] The description of the separation of the poor from the broader culture, and the influence of the "culture of poverty" upon the individual is attributed to Oscar Lewis. Before we examine each of the five dimensions of the culture of poverty ideal type, we should recall Lewis's statement:

> The culture of poverty . . . is not only an adaptation to a set of objective conditions of the larger society. Once it comes into existence it tends to perpetuate itself from generation to generation because of its effect on the children. By the time slum children are age six or seven they have usually absorbed the basic values and attitudes of their subculture and are not psychologically geared to take full advantage of changing conditions or increased opportunities which may occur in their lifetime.[22]

THE CULTURE OF POVERTY IDEAL TYPE

I. *The lower class possesses a distinct subculture manifest in deviant behaviors, values and focal concerns not present in the dominant culture; this subculture determines their socioeconomic status.*

Since Oscar Lewis is the author most frequently associated with the culture of poverty concept, we can turn to him for the development of this dimension of the ideal type. Lewis sees the culture of poverty emerging over time in response to the marginal position of the poor in a capitalistic, class-stratified society. Once in existence, the subculture takes on a behavioral system and set of values of its own. These adaptions to poverty, in turn, cause the poverty of following generations:

> In applying this concept of culture ("a design for living") to the understanding of poverty, I want to draw attention to the fact that

poverty in modern nations is not only a state of economic deprivation, of disorganization, or of the absence of something. It is also
something positive in the sense that it has a structure, a rationale,
and defense mechanisms without which the poor could hardly carry
on. In short, it is a way of life, remarkably stable and persistent,
passed down from generation to generation along family lines. The
culture of poverty has its own modalities and distinctive social and
psychological consequences for its members. It is a dynamic factor
which affects participation in the large national culture and becomes
a subculture of its own.[23]

While this statement relates to dimensions two, three, and four
of the ideal type, it is included here because it presents the
culture of poverty as a cohesive system. Whatever *initially*
caused the poor to be poor is no longer at issue, for the behaviors they adopted upon becoming poor and the values
which support those behaviors are what perpetuate their poverty. The way of life of the poor causes this group to remain
poor which, in turn, causes their children to be poor as the
young absorb the basic values and behaviors of the subculture.

Walter B. Miller sees this phenomena slightly differently.
He postulates that lower class values are an intentional reaction to the middle class, "a deliberate violation of middle
class norms."[24] The "focal concerns" of lower class youth
prevent them from being able to move out of the lower class.
Among those values cited by Miller are Trouble, Toughness,
Smartness (equivalent to "wit" or cunning as opposed to
knowledge in an intellectual sense), the need to create excite-
ment, a predetermined sense of fate, and an emphasis on Autonomy. These focal concerns form the basic interests of the
lower class delinquent gang; "The dominant component of
motivation underlying these (norm-violating) acts consists in
a directed attempt by the actor to adhere to forms of behavior,
and to achieve standards of value as they are defined within
that (lower class) community."[25] Having absorbed the values
and attitudes of their subculture, and learned the behavior

patterns, lower class children are psychologically unequipped to take advantage of opportunities to move out of poverty. The subcultural behavior patterns of the lower class supported by their value system thus cause the poor to remain poor.

II. *The major difference between the culture of poverty and the broader American culture is that the normative behavior patterns and values of the poverty culture deviate from those of the broader culture.*

The separate existence of the poverty subculture is postulated by the Council of Economic Advisers in its 1964 Annual Report: "The poor inhabit a world scarcely recognizable, and rarely recognized, by a majority of their fellow Americans. It is a world apart, whose inhabitants are isolated from the mainstream of American life and alienated from its values." [26] The position is reinforced by Walter B. Miller's contention: "There is a substantial segment of present-day American society whose way of life, values, and characteristic patterns of behavior are the product of a distinctive cultural system which may be termed 'lower class'." [27]

Oscar Lewis's studies of families in the culture of poverty describe the lack of organization among the poor and the failure of the poor to utilize the major institutions of the dominant culture: "The lack of effective participation and integration of the poor in the major institutions of the larger society is one of the crucial characteristics of the culture of poverty." [28] Among the institutions which the poor are divorced from is the labor force. Many theorists see this unemployment as a result of the deviant values of the lower class. According to Allison Davis, the culture of poverty does not allow the lower class child to learn "the 'ambition,' the drive for high skills, and for educational achievement that the middle class child learns in his family." [29] The extent of the schism between those living in a culture of poverty and those in the broader society is further illustrated by Oscar Lewis:

They have a low level of literacy and education, usually do not belong to labor unions, are not members of political parties, generally do not participate in the national welfare agencies, and make very little use of banks, hospitals, department stores, museums or art galleries. They have a critical attitude toward some of the basic institutions of the dominant classes, hatred of the police, mistrust of government and those in high position, and a cynicism which extends even to the church.[30]

This lower class behavior is the logical outcome of the existence of the subculture of poverty, just as middle class behavior is determined by being a part of the broader American culture. Unaffected by the goals, norms, and values of the broader society—in some cases, even unaware of it—the poor exist apart and isolated from conventional social life. In Oscar Lewis's conception, "People with a culture of poverty are provincial and locally oriented and have very little sense of history. They know only their own troubles, their own local conditions, their own neighborhood, their own way of life."[31]

III. *The poverty subculture constitutes a self-generating cycle, transmitted to children at an early age, and perpetuated both by the pattern of socialization to deviant behavior and values, and by the resultant psycho-social inadequacies which prohibit escape.*

The culture of poverty model provides a common meeting ground for believers in psychological determinism and impaired socialization. As indicated in passages from Lewis and Miller, among others, the socialization of the young child into the life-ways or culture of poverty psychologically limits his capacity to take advantage of opportunities available in the broader society.

Those with a psychological approach to understanding the problems of poverty perceive the behaviors of the poor as pathological, and focus more particularly on their child-rearing practices. In his now famous *Report on the Negro Family,*

Moynihan was explicit in describing "the tangle of pathology," and the detrimental impact of the culture of poverty upon the young. In developing this assertion, Moynihan is known to have been influenced by E. Franklin Frazier, whom he quotes:

As the result of family disorganization a large proportion of Negro children and youth have not undergone the socialization which only the family can provide. The disorganized families have failed to provide for their emotional needs and have not provided the discipline and habits which are necessary for personality development. Because the disorganized family has failed in its function as a socializing agency, it has handicapped the children in their relations to the institutions in the community.[32]

Other harmful effects said to be incurred by lower class children because of class differentiated child-rearing practices include the following:

The poor are less likely to encourage a child's interest in exploration, discovery, inquiry; they are more likely to reward inactivity and passivity as attributes of a "good child"; they are less likely to enhance and reward development of verbal skills through precept and approval; they are more likely to display repressive and punitive attitudes towards sex, sex questioning and experimentation, and a view of the sex relationship as basically exploitive; they are more likely to rely on authoritarian methods of child rearing; they are more likely to discipline by corporal punishment, harshly and inconsistently applied.[33]

Because these and other traits are assumed to be passed on from one generation to the next, the culture of poverty is portrayed as constituting a design for living which becomes "the cycle of poverty." The cyclical aspects derive from the assumption that the behaviors and values of the poor are the independent variables and their poverty is the dependent variable. When the behaviors and values are transmitted to the children, the major cause of poverty is therefore also transmitted.

IV. *The poverty subculture must be eliminated and the poor assimilated to middle or working class value patterns before poverty itself can be done away with.*

The reduction or elimination of poverty, according to the derived ideas aggregated under the culture of poverty, must begin by focusing on the changes which the poor must make to move upward in the occupational system. Since the poverty subculture is composed of deviant behavior patterns supported by value systems distinctly different from those of the middle class, the starting point for positive action must be the reduction or elimination of this deviant belief system. It is assumed that people born into a poverty subculture could not by themselves take advantage of available opportunity. Therefore, programs geared toward resolution of the problem must focus on the individual's behavior and his value system, and on offering different or alternative values to the young.

To improve the underprivileged worker's performance, one must help him to learn to want and to be anxious to attain higher goals for himself and for his children. . . . The problem of changing the work habits and motivation of people who come out of families like the (X's) is far more complex than mere supervision and pressure. It is a problem of changing the goals, the ambitions, and the level of cultural and occupational aspiration of the underprivileged worker.[34]

This statement draws specific implications from both Lewis and Miller that the cultural standards of the poor are more important to their condition than their poverty; consequently these standards must receive the highest priority in planning and programming.

Alexander Leighton also expresses concern for the ordering of priorities, and is explicit about the notion that poverty itself may be easier to eliminate than the culture of poverty:

Clearly increased economic and educational opportunities will not be enough to bring about a turn for the better in a disintegrated community, although such opportunities are essential to the process. What is needed in addition to them is the development of patterns of social functioning: leadership, followership and practice in acting together cooperatively . . . Rooted in this necessity is the requirement that the people be enabled to gain confidence that some things can be done to better their lot; that they be assisted in modifying unrealistic or nihilistic views of the world, and that they be encouraged to develop motivation. Without social and psychological changes of this kind the people will retain their inability to make adequate use of educational and employment opportunities.[35]

The next section, devoted to explicating more fully the course of action which derives from the culture of poverty theory, attempts to take suggestions made by Leighton, Davis or the other authors included under this ideal type and mold them into a strategy of social action. In effect, it is intended to answer the question, "What would you do about poverty?", or "How would you go about eliminating poverty?", given the position taken on its causes and characteristics as noted in this chapter.

V. *In contemporary American society, the elimination of poverty can be accomplished through directed culture change, social work and psychiatric therapies, and compensatory education.*

Based on the culture of poverty theme of deviant behavior supported by a defective value system, programs created out of the individual and cultural change strategy will be designed to: 1) provide counselling or therapy to help the individual or small groups of individuals modify their behavior to adjust to societal expectations; 2) assist individuals or small groups to make full use of the existing institutions of the society such as social agencies, the school system, hospitals, etc.; and 3) focus on remedying the handicaps which naturally derive from cultural disadvantage.

Lee Rainwater, in describing this type of social service-compensatory education strategy, notes its assumption "that the poor can be changed while they are still poor, and that once they have changed, they will then be able to (function) in ways that will do away with their poverty."[36] The services offered through this strategy can be described as rehabilitative, seeking to change the person while accepting his environment as it is. Examples of such programs would include clinical social work and mental health counselling, family life education, planned parenthood, vocational counselling, group therapy and group work (although this approximates the third type of program, that related to cultural disadvantage).

The second type of program deriving from this explanation of the problem is based on the assumption that the poor do not make use of existing institutions. These programs include information and referral; neighborhood centers which provide the same services as the traditional agencies but are decentralized into the neighborhoods where the poor reside; and efforts to organize inhabitants of poor communities to engender support for existing or newly created services, and enrichment or remedial programs.

The compensatory education-cultural enrichment programs are based on the assumption that the special educational problems of the poor (such as dropping out of school, underachievement, lack of motivation) can be resolved through remedial approaches. Programs which provide more reading teachers, lower class size, special materials, additional guidance counselors and earlier exposure to the school setting all focus on assisting the lower class child in accommodating himself to the behavioral and educational standards of the school.[37] The compensatory education programs derived from this ideal type exist for all age groups: pre-school programs such as Head Start for the very young; tutorial or intensified programs throughout the primary and secondary schools (for example, the Higher Horizons or More Effective Schools programs in New York); and, for adults, programs of adult education or vocational education to upgrade the skill levels of the unemployed. Often associated with these formal educational programs are programs of cultural enrichment.

All of these programs concentrate on the individual, small groups of individuals or a subcultural environment as the focus for change. This focus is the logical derivative of the culture of poverty definition of the problem.

NOTES

[1] Hunter, Robert, *Poverty* (New York City: MacMillan Company, 1912), pp. 3–4.

[2] Leighton, Alexander H., "Poverty and Social Change," in *The Scientific American*, Vol. 212 No. 5 (May 1965), p. 23.

[3] Matza, David, "The Disreputable Poor," in *Class, Status, and Power* (Second Edition), Seymour Martin Lipset and Reinhard Bendix, eds. (New York: The Free Press (1966), p. 290.

[4] Quoted in David Macarov, *Incentives to Work: The Effect of Unearned Income*, (Unpublished Ph.D. thesis, Florence Heller Graduate School for Advanced Studies in Social Welfare, Brandeis University, Waltham, Massachusetts (1968), p. 116.

[5] Hyman, H. H., (in Lipset and Bendix, eds., *Class, Status, and Power*), p. 488.

[6] *Ibid*, p. 490.

[7] *Ibid*, p. 492.

[8] *Ibid*, p. 494.

[9] Brown, Gordon E., ed., *The Multi-Problem Dilemma*, (Matuchen, N.J.: Scarecrow Press (1968), p. 9.

[10] New York City Youth Board, *Reaching the Unreached Family: A Study of Service to Families and Children*, 1958.

[11] *Report of the Multi-Problem Family Committee*, Family and Child Welfare Section, Community Welfare Council, Rockford, Illinois, 1958.

[12] Montgomery, George W., "Reaching the Hard Core Family," paper presented at the New York State Welfare Conference, Rochester, New York, 1957.

[13] Community Development Program of Oneida County, Executive Director's Final Report (June 30, 1959), p. 12.

[14] *Report on Hard-to-Reach Multi-Problem Families*, Family and Children's Division, Council of Social Agencies of Rochester and Monroe County (dated November 25, 1959), p. 2.

[15] Hallinan, Helen W., "Coordinating Agency Efforts in Behalf of the Hard-to-Reach Family," *Social Casework*, (January 1959), p. 9.

[16] *Multi-Problem Families: A New Name or a New Problem?*, New York State Charities Aid Association (May 1960), p. 3.

[17] *Ibid*, p. 4.

[18] Office of Policy Planning and Research, United States Department of Labor, *The Negro Family: The Case for National Action*, pp. 29–30.

[19] Council of Economic Advisers, *Economic Report of the President — 1964*, (Washington, D. C.: U.S. Government Printing Office, 1964), p. 69.

[20] Miller, Walter B., "Lower Class Culture as a Generating Milieu of Gang Delinquency," *Journal of Social Issues*, Vol. XIV No. 3 (1958), p. 5.

[21] Miller, Walter B., "Implications of Urban Lower-Class Culture for Social Work," *Social Service Review*, Vol. XXXIII No. 3 (September 1959), p. 219.

[22] Lewis, Oscar, *La Vida* (New York: Random House, 1966), p. xiv.

[23] Lewis, Oscar, *Children of Sanchez* (New York: Random House, 1961), p. xxiv.

[24] Miller, W. B., "Lower-Class Culture . . .", p. 6.

[25] *Ibid*, p. 5.

[26] Council of Economic Advisers, p. 55.

[27] Miller, W. B., "Lower-Class Culture . . .", p. 6.

[28] Lewis, *La Vida*, p. xiv.

[29] Davis, Allison, "The Motivation of the Underprivileged Worker," in *Industry and Society*, William Foote Whyte, ed. (New York and London: McGraw-Hill Book Company, Inc., 1946), p. 89.

[30] Lewis, *La Vida*, pp. xlv–xlvi.

[31] *Ibid*, p. xlviii.

[32] Frazier, E. Franklin, "Problems and Needs of Negro Children and Youth Resulting from Family Disorganization," *Journal of Negro Education* (Summer 1950), pp. 276–277.

[33] Lewis, Hylan, "Agenda Paper No. V: The Family: Resources for Change — Planning Session for the White House Conference 'To Fulfill These Rights,'" in Lee Rainwater and William L. Yancy, *The Moynihan Report and the Politics of Controversy*, (Cambridge: The MIT Press, 1967), p. 336.

[34] Davis, "The Motivation of the Underprivileged Worker," p. 90.

[35] Leighton, "Poverty and Social Change," p. 27.

[36] Rainwater, Lee, "The Services Strategy vs. the Income Strategy," *Trans-action*, Vol. 4, No. 10 (October 1967), p. 41.

[37] Fantini, Mario D., "Beyond Cultural Deprivation and Compensatory Education," *Psychiatry and Social Service Review*, Vol. 3 No. 6, pp. 9–10.

CHAPTER IV

The Dysfunctional Social System

JUST as the preceding ideal type had two orienting concepts, the dysfunctional social system model contains two basic assumptions: the existence of "social facts," and the influence of these social facts upon human behavior. These two assertions are derived from Durkheim who emphasizes the significance of society as a construct, rather than as a vast aggregate of individuals. The construct of society, of phenomena existing outside or beyond individuals, is based on the premise of "social facts," or ways of acting which can exercise external constraint on the individual, or which are general throughout a society.[1]

Durkheim assumes that in the interaction between people certain negotiated arrangements are worked out which influence—constrain or control—the behaviors of the individuals involved. The arrangements eventually become patterned around the density, the purpose, and the context of the interaction. In a densely populated, complex industrialized society, institutions emerge to regulate interaction between groups and individuals. This patterned interaction, with its attendant institutions is defined as the social system or the social structure.

In *Social Theory and Social Structure*, Robert Merton postulates that the social system has two intimately related component parts, the cultural structure and the social structure, which form the individual's salient environment: the cultural structure is the organized set of normative values governing behavior which are common to members in a given society; and the social structure is the organized set of social relationships

in which members of the society are implicated.[2] Merton
assumes a hierarchical arrangement of people aggregated into
social classes. One should note that in this conception the same
cultural structure pertains to all individuals within the social
structure regardless of their position in the hierarchy of social
classes.

The cultural structure contains societally defined goals,
values, purposes, and interests, of things "worth striving for,"
which are "held out as legitimate objectives for all." The cultural structure also "defines, regulates, and controls the acceptable modes of reaching out for these goals."[3] The channels
or paths to attain culturally prescribed goals, however, are
regulated by the social structure, which imposes barriers in a
non-random manner to individuals and groups within the social
system.

. . . the social structure strains the cultural values, making action in
accord with them readily possible for those occupying certain sta-
tuses within the society and difficult or impossible for others. The
social structure acts as a barrier or as an open door to the acting out
of cultural mandates.[4]

Linton defines status as a set of rights and duties distinct
from the individual who occupies it, and to which an individual
is socially assigned.[5] For Merton, the allocation of status within
a society is determined by one's location within the social
hierarchy. Thus, higher status will be conferred within the
cultural structure to those at the top. This group, in turn, is
made up of the individuals who have access to legitimate
means of achieving culturally prescribed goals. Others, assigned to lower status positions within the social structure, are
denied access both to the legitimate means for achieving the
culturally designated goals and, unless they become deviant
by going outside the prescribed means, are therefore denied
access to the goals of the culture.

Merton extends this theoretical position to explain deviant

behavior on a mass scale as the result of extolling certain culturally approved success goals for an entire population while structurally denying a large portion of that same population access to approved modes of attaining those goals.[6] The dysfunctional social system explanatory model absorbs Merton's central hypothesis: deviant behavior results from an imposed contradiction between culturally prescribed aspirations and socially structured access routes.

Merton's hypothesis is adopted as an explanatory scheme by Richard Cloward and Lloyd Ohlin in *Delinquency and Opportunity.*[7] In essence, they argue that delinquency among lower class youth arises when serious discrepancies exist between aspirations for success and opportunities for gaining it. Opportunity theory, as their position has become popularly known, led to the development of a large-scale program to combat juvenile delinquency. At its core lies the assumption that the social structure was the cause of the social problem of delinquency:

What we have been saying only points up all the more the fallacy of attributing delinquent responses in the lower class to inadequate socialization or simply to conformity with lower-class values. One can accept these perspectives only if it is assumed either that the lower class is highly disorganized and demoralized or that a large number of lower-class persons are unacculturated to the system of norms that prevails in our society generally. We contend, on the other hand, that widespread tendencies toward delinquent practices in the lower class are modes of adaptation to structured strains and inconsistencies within the social order.[8]

The disjuncture between prescribed goals and imposed obstacles to accomplishing them becomes all the more complex, given the importance of the success-achievement goals in America. Central to the success-achievement goal is financial gain, of making money.

Differential location within the social structure discriminately allocates resources and provides access to those resources to restricted numbers of people, while at the same time equally saturating all social strata with the culturally approved goals; the most salient of these is the accumulation of wealth. This malintegration of cultural goals and social structure can be seen as creating poverty (the way the structure is organized), and indirectly causing deviant behavior (by pervasive diffusion of the cultural goals) as a response to resulting frustration.

THE DYSFUNCTIONAL SOCIAL SYSTEM IDEAL TYPE

I. *The lower class forms a distinct subsociety manifest in deprived socio-economic circumstances which result from a dysfunctional social structure.*

Prevailing American ideology, focused on the culturally prescribed goals of monetary success, the open-classed society, and the work ethic, was forced to reconsider its own mythology for a time. The time was the great depression. Over fourteen million workers were unemployed, and explanations of this situation based on low motivation, low ambition, or moral deviation were obviously inappropriate. There were no opportunities in any area of the economy.

The vulnerability of the worker to the national social structure and its dysfunction was made clear, but became almost obliterated with the economic recovery during and after the Second World War. Once again, the historical American belief system was perpetuated, exaggerating false notions of rugged individualism, rapid upward mobility, and a fluid social system abounding with opportunities for all.

The ready re-acceptance of an ideology proven fallible by the Great Depression is explained by the perpetuation of three cultural axioms in the society. Merton describes these axioms:

First, all should strive for the same lofty goals since these are open to all; second, present seeming failure is but a way-station to ultimate success; and third, genuine failure consists only in the lessening or withdrawal of ambition.[9]

He goes on to explain that each of these cultural axioms has a different sociological meaning, but they all serve the same function of assuring the American populace of the sanctity of the existing system. The first axiom deflects criticism from the structure of economic and political organization onto those individuals who are victimized by that structure; the second axiom preserves the distribution of power by having individuals in the lower strata identify themselves with those at the top (where the lower class may some day make its way); while the third axiom locates responsibility for failure on those individuals who are portrayed as refusing to conform to cultural dictates.[10]

The theme of a prevailing American ideology, saturated with the work ethic and its related values, is also noted by Elinor Graham. The American business creed has infused the cultural perspective with its image of the interaction between the individual and the corporate structure. An idealized "free-enterprise" system creates the possibility for fusion between dream and actuality by perpetrating the myth of national wealth as the product of atomized individuals whose labor and opportunities are maximized by a "free competitive market" system.[11] Graham contends that poverty became a political issue because it served the political interests of the existing administration, rather than the interests of those persons who have been relegated by the social structure to the lower economic strata.

Non-accidental visability of the poor in more affluent societies, is explained by George Simmel:

. . . assistance (to the poor) is based on the structure of society, whatever it may be . . . The goal of assistance is precisely to mitigate certain extreme manifestations of social differentiation, so that the social structure may continue to be based on this differentiation.[12]

Lewis Coser later pursued the theme of the equilibrium maintaining motivation for societal actions "beneficial" to the poor. He went further, however, in describing the absence of choice involved in becoming poor for most people who are categorized as poor as a result of society reacting to them in a particular manner. This societal attribution clearly outweighs any of the heterogeneity of origins or characteristics found among the poor. Coser concludes that, in contrast to all other strata, the poor are a social category "not by virtue of what they do, but by virtue of what is done to them." [13]

Being acted upon by forces beyond one's control, being arbitrarily relegated to an unfavorable status and being maintained there by circumstances (the working of the social structure) which appear unrelated to one's interests or even the interests of the total society, form the essence of the social structure ideal type.

S. M. Miller and Martin Rein, whose concepts about social action strategies will be discussed below, articulate the dysfunction of the social system. They argue that people who have an unprotected structural relationship to our political and economic system become victimized by it as new conditions emerge. Citing the aged who were not poor during their "productive" lives, Miller and Rein point out the vulnerability of all seemingly enfranchised workers to such forces as automation.[14] Hyman Lumer illustrates the impact of automation on two other groups of workers, the Appalachian coal miners and Pittsburgh steelworkers, who certainly did not become poor as a result of either low motivation or low productivity. Rather, it is the multiplication of the worker's productivity by machine and the utilization of that machine by the employers which made casualties of the miners and steelworkers. Lumer emphasizes the fact that the recent poverty of these groups is absolutely unrelated to their personal characteristics or values. Individual differences can only determine which people or groups are most likely to be poor—given the continued existence of poverty as a social condition in society.[15]

Along with numerous others as divergent as Stokely Carmichael and the United States Civil Rights Commission, Lumer
thoroughly documents the existence of racial discrimination
throughout the social structure of America. The systemically
imposed inequities in the attainment of the cultural goals of
society are evidenced in data on employment,[16] education,[17]
health care,[18] and welfare services.[19] In many areas, however,
data on race are available without any control for income as
a potentially significant variable. This is not an attempt to dis-
count racial discrimination and race prejudice as pervasive
phenomena in American life; rather it questions whether sufficient data has been collected using social class as a control
variable. It is beyond the scope of this work to examine this
issue in any greater depth, but the neglect of social class in
relation to the achievement of cultural goals is rarely mentioned. Where social class is a focus of concern, the substance
of most studies is often on class differentiated values—class
related differences in adherence to the cultural norms of the
broader society. This issue of values and cultural affiliation
leads to the second dimension of the ideal type.

II. *The distinctive behavior patterns of the poor are normal
adaptations to the frustration which comes from adherence to
the cultural goals and values of a broader society in which the
social structure imposes barriers to goal attainment.*

The structural ideal type posits an entirely different position,
one which contradicts the culture of poverty framework explaining this dimension. The culture of poverty model explains
distinctive behavioral patterns among the lower class as derivative from an omnipresent subcultural value system. The structural explanatory model, in contrast, attributes lower class
related life styles directly to the adherence by lower class
persons to the broader cultural structure, its values, goals, and
prescribed pathways. Merton analyzes deviant behavior among
the lower class as an adaptive result of the frustration which

follows when cultural allegiance is thwarted by structurally imposed barriers to goal attainment. We may take the position of the structural model here from Charles Valentine:

> The distinctive patterns of social life at the lowest income levels are determined by structural conditions of the larger society beyond the control of low-income people, not by socialization in primary groups committed to a separate cultural design. Otherwise stated, the design for living received by the poor through socialization is not significantly distinct from that of the society as a whole, but the actual conditions of low-income life are importantly inconsistent with actualization of this cultural design.[20]

In an analytic account of Black streetcorner men, Elliot Liebow describes the process of making existential adaptations to structurally imposed obstacles to the success goals of the broader culture. His intensive study also documents the commitment of these men to the goals and values of the broader society. Of greatest importance to the cultural structure, according to Merton and others, its the work ethic as a foundation of the success-achievement value in American society. Liebow, describing the imposed marginal relationship of the streetcorner man to the labor market, makes note of the relationship between belief in the broader value system and an externally enforced marginal status.

The streetcorner man, for example, places the same value on the jobs available to him as the larger social milieu which surrounds him. He estimates that value by the nature of the work he is given and the wage level offered to him. Despite the low status, low pay nature of work—which both the employer and the worker acknowledge—the streetcorner man is ostracized for failing to diligently perform tasks at a wage level inadequate to support his family.[21] Valentine found that Liebow's major contribution to the study of low income life-styles is his documentation of the total sense of personal failure which pervades the lives of streetcorner men *because these men share the beliefs, standards and values of the broader culture.*[22]

In order to determine the degree to which lower class persons subscribed to the values of the dominant culture, Hylan Lewis and his associates undertook a large-scale study in Washington, D. C. Lewis concludes that

> . . . erosion and failure in many poor families are due less to the lack of recognition of, and affirmation of, so-called middle class values than to the wherewithal to support these values and to afford the tastes and wishes that inextricably bind the poor to the larger society. The tragedy of most of the poor parents . . . is the unremitting tension created by the gap between their desires, particularly for their children, and their ability to fulfill these desires.[23]

Lewis concludes that the values, the preferred living patterns, and the desires of the lower class parallel those of the middle class. His work is supported by Liebow, who documents the relationship between marginality in the work force and lack of stability in marriage. Failure in work, pre-ordained for the lower class male, does not allow him to support his family adequately, which he often deserts in self-defense. He tries to protect himself from the overwhelming sense of failure which permeates his life, but there can be no escape so long as the lower class male adheres to the cultural structure of the broader society. Marriage thus reflects the structurally imposed impoverishment of the lower class male, destroying his family life as it destroyed his sense of adequacy as a human being. One common response to account for this perpetual crush, based on Merton's cultural axioms, is the development of concepts of class-determined behavior patterns or life styles parallel to those used by culture of poverty theorists.

Hylan Lewis, on the basis of his research, cautions the middle class observer of these distinctive behavior patterns that it is important not to confuse *observed* behavior with *preferred* patterns of living. After carrying out a comparative study of child rearing values and practices, he concludes

(a) The actual behaviors of low-income people are not to be confused with their values and aspirations.

(b) Urban low-income families reflect a complex of behaviors and goals which include both adaptation to impoverishment and desired socio-economic status.

(c) Parents in low-income families show greater conformity to middle and upper class standards in their value preferences and goals than in their behaviors.

(d) The child-rearing concerns of the lower class closely approximate those ascribed to middle and upper income groups.

(e) With few exceptions, low income parents do not prefer or approve of the conditions in which they and their children exist.

(f) A major goal of low income parents is that their children do better in all aspects of life than they have done themselves.[24]

The overriding judgment derived from these studies is that, despite perpetual frustration, the lower class abides by the cultural dictates of the broader society, and in so doing continues to suffer a sustained sense of failure and inadequacy which results from structurally determined immobility existing in concert with cultural assimilation.

Hyman Rodman has described the ability of the lower class to exist with the frustration, the overtly deviant behavior patterns, and the adherence to cultural norms as "the lower class value stretch." His concept describes the broader value range of the lower class which appends to those values they share with middle and upper strata an alternative set of values or a stretching of standardized values which allow the poor to adapt to their impoverishment.[25] Liebow has developed a similar concept, "shadow values," which refines Rodman's ideas.

Shadow values are acknowledged to be of less importance and receive less commitment from streetcorner men because the men are aware, ultimately, that these shadow values are ersatz, created to substitute for the real thing in view of overwhelming circumstances. Liebow further develops the concept of shadow values:

. . . they are derivative, subsidiary in nature, thinner and less weighty, less completely internalized, and seem to be value images reflected by forced or adaptive behavior rather than real values with a positive determining influence on behavior of choice . . .

. . . the alternative value system is not a distinct value system which can be separately invoked by the users. It appears only in association with the parent system and is separable from it only analytically. Derivative, insubstantial, and co-curring with the parent system, it is as if the alternative value system is a shadow cast by the common value system in the distorting lower-class setting.[26]

Thus, one may conclude that the distinctive behavior patterns among the lower class are existential adaptations to the circumstances in which they are forced to live, with deviant behavior resulting from the internal conflict between cultural affiliation and alienation from the social structural benefit system.

III. *The structural position and subsocietal behavior patterns of the poor stem from historical and contemporary sources which generally involve multiple factors including lack of access to the political and economic systems, systematic racial discrimination, and ineffective social institutions which prohibit rather than facilitate full participation in the larger society.*

The social structuralist position on this dimension is on the perpetuation of specific groups of individuals at the bottom of the status hierarchy within American society. Deviant behavior or class specific behavior does not occur as the result of a pre-deterministic socialization to pathological lifeways or as the result of being reared in a multi-problem family. These patterns arise, rather, because the poor must continually adapt to a social situation which is constantly oppressive in its imposed barriers to culturally prescribed goal attainment. Lee Rainwater has pointed out this process of working out self-protective adaptations for succeeding generations of the oppressed: each generation of poor people learns both the survival skills necessary to exist and the normative standards of the broader society.[27]

Liebow's conclusions from his study of streetcorner men further establish that continuity in deviance is permanence in societally imposed or structured failure patterns:

... the streetcorner man does not appear as a carrier of an independent cultural tradition. His behavior appears not so much as a way of realizing the distinctive goals and values of his own subculture, or of conforming to its models, but rather as his way of trying to achieve many of the goals and values of the larger society, of failing to do this, and of concealing his failure from others and from himself as best he can. . . .

... We do not have to see the problem in terms of breaking into a puncture proof circle, of trying to change values, of disrupting the lines of communication between parent and child so that parents cannot make children in their own image, thereby transmitting their culture inexorably, ad infinitum . . . Of much greater importance . . . is the fact that many similarities between the lower class Negro father and son (or mother and daughter) do not result from "cultural transmission" but from the fact that the son goes out and independently experiences the same failures, in the same areas, and for much the same reasons as his father.[28]

The perpetual existence of overt racial discrimination in American society, with its attendant behavior inducing characteristics, is often mistaken for the existence of a subculture. Valentine is harshly critical of those who confuse the difference between statistical data (census and court records) with cultural configurations. He notes that census figures tell nothing about the structures and processes of a culture; they merely report a "demographic reality." [29]

The demographic reality for all the poor, and particularly for those of racial minority, is one of deprivation imposed with unstinting regularity by the social structure of American society.

The most recent resource file on the creation of ghettoes in city after city across our nation is a document produced by The National Advisory Commission on Civil Disorders. Commonly known as the "Kerner Commission," the group of men selected for membership—none of them known for any particularly radical political activity in relation to the problems of race in American life—produced a remarkable document. Their report is notable primarily because it sees the problems of black people in American society as a result of the white controlled social structure:

Segregation and poverty have created in the racial ghetto a destructive environment totally unknown to most white Americans.

What white Americans have never fully understood — but what the Negro can never forget — is that white society is deeply implicated in the ghetto. White institutions created it, white institutions maintain it, and white society condones it. [30]

The Report is massive, covering all phases of life as life has come to be divided among the institutions which have emerged to provide needed services for the complex industrialized urban community. Listed as sources of trouble are the areas of employment, housing, crime and insecurity, health and sanitation conditions, and exploitation of consumers. The Commission leaves little doubt as to the source of the problem.

While the Commission documents the failure of the institutions of the larger society to eliminate the poverty and discrimination toward the racial minorities, others have critically examined the capacity of the institutions to deal with all the poor. In large part, administrative bureaucrats have responded negatively to the poor whose lives they affect. The officials' attitude corresponds to the prevailing ideology, which interprets poverty as the result of individual rather than systemic defect. Discussing the way in which the so-called "helping" institutions can create and perpetuate the problem of poverty, Martin Rein describes the discrimination against people from low income backgrounds as built into the procedures of social service bureaucracies—including the public school system. His criticism focuses on standards of appearance and performance which derive from the ethics and values of business and industrial production. Low income people are compared to role models which stereotype middle class behavior patterns, with those people who fit the model being encouraged to move ahead, while others are denied access to training and educational experiences.

To describe poverty as a cycle or to talk of inter-generational poverty is to mistake description for analysis. While the children of the poor are often poor, while the behavior patterns are statistically more often deviant, the structure and circumstances of life as they affect the poor retain their intractability as well. What passes for permanent states of being among the poor is in fact a continued effort to adjust to an unjust social order. The necessary changes, as described in the next section, will consequently have to be in the social system rather than within a subgroup of the population affected by that system.

IV. *To eliminate poverty, two changes have to be brought about simultaneously: alterations of the social structure to ensure open access to economic opportunity, and increased power for the poor vis-à-vis the institutions which affect their lives.*

Since this chapter began with Merton's analysis of the structural implication in the existence of poverty, it is appropriate to return to Merton for the rationale for the strategy which follows from this perspective:

. . . it is plain that differential pressures for deviant behavior will continue to be exerted upon certain groups and strata only as long as the structure of opportunity and the cultural goals remain substantially unchanged. Correlatively, as significant changes in the structure or goals occur, we should expect corresponding changes in the sectors of the population most severely exposed to these pressures.[31]

Bringing about change in the structure—whether social or cultural—of the society has *not* been a focus of efforts to eliminate poverty in America. Rather, efforts at change have been related to poverty stricken individuals, who were considered the source of their own misfortune. This latter approach is consistent with the cultural structure and its explanations of the problems of poverty. That people are unable to acknowledge the structurally imposed inferior position of others is not surprising, given the overwhelming saturation of the society's cultural axioms. The dominance of the work ethic, with associated beliefs in individual motivation and access to upward mobility, prevents people from understanding the inherent inequities in our economic and political system. Cases which appear to validate the mythology of hard work and access to the systemic reward system are tokens serving to perpetuate the cultural standards.

The focus of a strategy to eliminate poverty, from the perspective of the dysfunctional social system ideal type, *is contradictory* to tokenism. This strategy begins by assessing defects in the social structure, and logically leads to an action program designed to change that social structure. Structural change advocates clearly specify that continued social programming which focuses on the individual adversely affected by the social structure is nothing more than political behavior aimed at maintaining existing power relationships in the society.[32] They note that these power arrangements, which keep the structure functioning in an unjust manner, are to be the focal point for change efforts. In *The Democratic Man*, Edward Lindeman concludes,

The social diagnostician who places all of the blame for maladjustment on the individual and none upon the social order must in the end become servile to those whose interests are vested in that order. He must, in short, become a tool of the power groups.[33]

With the emphasis on social change rather than individual rehabilitation, the broad policy outline which emerges from this approach is directed at changes in the political, economic and social structures. More specifically, the strategy calls for reallocation of political power, lowering the concentration of power held by the upper classes and used to promote their interests; for reallocation of the nation's economic benefits involving a redistribution of wealth and resources; and, for a reallocation of the roles and status assignments, altering the segments of the population which are assigned to the higher status positions. Since these profound changes politically threaten the established organizational relationships in a society, the traditional agencies entrusted to administer social welfare programs cannot be expected to respond adequately to the demands of this strategy. These agencies should not be responsible for programs directed toward the goals specified above.

The emphasis on innovation in organizational structures as well as in programs reflects the position that many of the agencies supposedly created to serve the poor have in fact contributed to their exploitation. The following comment serves as a mild example of this approach:

Existing service-dispensing institutions have failed to alter the relative position of the disadvantaged. Many social institutions have ignored or dealt inadequately with the poor. Therefore, it will not be sufficient to simply provide these institutions of failure with more funds — to continue doing what they have always done in the past. It is necessary to change social institutions so that they are more effectively responsible to the needs of the poor. Changes in the programs of educational and welfare institutions and in the styles of professional intervention are needed.[34]

Specific programs designed as part of this overall strategy of social change are discussed in more detail in the next section.

V. *In contemporary American society, the most likely source for the changes necessary to eliminate poverty lies in the organization of the poor to exercise political power, to participate in the planning and administration of relevant programs, and in increasing control by the poor over the institutions which are instrumental in their lives.*

Programs which derive from the social structural ideal type and its institutional change strategy must take into account both the participation of the poor in making critical decisions *and* the social structure as the focus of efforts at change. Of immediate importance is the organization of the poor into groups which can be mobilized to take collective action on their own behalf. Community organization programs, attempts to develop unions among the non-unionized low income workers in standard jobs, developing community based political parties, and setting up self-managed non-profit corporations which benefit all members of the low income community are all examples of this type of structural change orientation.

Since changing roles and status allocation, or changing the population eligible for certain status, also follows from the social structural explanatory model, programs serving this function are included under the structural change strategy. Such programs might include New Careers programs in the service professions which alter the necessary credentials and the concepts of appropriate appearances which previously were exclusively the prerogatives of various professional groups. Other programs which emphasize the commitment of various industries to employ and to train low income people while providing them with subsidized education are within the institutional change strategy, as are programs which are geared toward community economic development.

Concerning these various efforts at change, however, one should recall that the old-line community institutions are not capable of altering the structure. As a result, another vital program aspect would be the development of self-managed corporations (necessarily non-profit, or based on a system where any profit which accrued was redistributed to benefit the community rather than a small subsection of the residents). The commitment to political action is essential, since any organization set up to benefit poor people by performing relevant functions for them would compete with already existing organizations managed by the other social strata and serving their interests. Thus, for any program which follows the dictates of structural change strategy, we must anticipate conflict.

All of the programs mentioned here have in common the focus on the social structure as the object of change. They derive from the ideal type in that the social system is dysfunctional, creating and perpetuating severe problems for a large portion of society.

NOTES

[1] Durkheim, Emile, *The Rules of Sociological Method,* translated by Sara Solovay, et al. (New York: The Free Press, 1964), p. 13.

[2] Merton, Robert K., *Social Theory and Social Structure* (Revised and Enlarged Edition), (Glencoe: The Free Press, 1957), pp. 162–163.

[3] *Ibid,* p. 134.

[4] *Ibid,* pp. 162–163.

[5] Linton, Ralph, *The Study of Man,* (New York: Appleton-Century-Crofts, 1936), p. 113.

[6] Merton, *Social Theory and Social Structure,* p. 146.

[7] Cloward, Richard A., and Ohlin, Lloyd E., *Delinquency and Opportunity* (Glencoe: The Free Press, 1960).

[8] Cloward and Ohlin, *Delinquency and Opportunity,* p. 106.

[9] Merton, *Social Theory and Social Structure,* p. 139.

[10] *Ibid,* p. 139.

[11] Graham, Elinor, "The Politics of Poverty," in *Poverty As A Public Issue*, Ben B. Seligman, ed. (New York: The Free Press, 1965), pp. 237–238.

[12] Simmel, George, "The Poor," *Social Problems*, Vol. 13 No. 2, (Fall, 1965), p. 122.

[13] Coser, Lewis A., "The Sociology of Poverty," *Social Problems*, Vol. 13 No. 2 (Fall, 1965), p. 142.

[14] Miller, S. M. and Rein, Martin, "The War on Poverty: Perspectives and Prospects," in *Poverty as a Public Issue*, Ben B. Seligman, (New York: The Free Press, 1965), pp. 237–238.

[15] Lumer, Hyman, *Poverty: Its Roots and Its Future*, (New York: International Publishers, 1965), p. 16.

[16] Hill, Herbert, "Racial Inequality in Employment — The Patterns of Discrimination," in *The Annals of the American Academy of Political and Social Science*, Vol. 357 (January 1965).

[17] *Equality of Education Opportunity*, United States Department of Health, Education, and Welfare, 1966.

[18] *Report of the National Advisory Commission on Civil Disorders*, (Toronto and New York: Bantam Books Inc., 1968), pp. 269–274.

[19] Silberman, Charles E., *Crisis in Black and White*, (New York: Random House, 1964), see especially Chapter X, "The Revolt Against Welfare Colonialism."

[20] Valentine, Charles A., *Culture and Poverty*, (Chicago: University of Chicago Press, 1968), p. 129.

[21] Liebow, Elliot, *Tally's Corner: A Study of Negro Streetcorner Men*, (Boston: Little, Brown and Company, 1967), pp. 57–60.

[22] Valentine, *Culture and Poverty*, p. 97.

[23] Lewis, Hylan, *Perspectives on Poverty: A Study Manual*, p. 116.

[24] Lewis, Hylan, "The Family: Resources for Change," Agenda Paper No. V from the White House Conference, "To Fulfill These Rights," in *The Moynihan Report and the Politics of Controversy*, Lee Rainwater and William L. Yancy, (Cambridge: The M.I.T. Press, 1967), pp. 336–338.

[25] Rodman, Hyman, "The Lower Class Value Stretch," *Social Forces*, Vol. 42 No. 2 (December 1963), p. 209.

[26] Liebow, *Tally's Corner*, p. 213, footnote 3.

[27] Rainwater, Lee, "The Problem of Lower Class Culture," (Pruitt-Igoe Occasional Paper Number 8 — mimeographed), p. 35.

[28] Liebow, *Tally's Corner*, pp. 221–223.

[29] Valentine, *Culture and Poverty*, p. 6.

[30] *Report of the National Advisory Commission on Civil Disorders*, (Bantam Books; Toronto, New York, London — 1968), p. 2.

[31] Merton, *Social Theory and Social Structure*, p. 192.

[32] Walinsky, Adam, "Keeping the Poor in Their Place: Notes on the Importance of Being One-up," in *New Perspectives on Poverty*, Arthur B. Shostak and William Gomberg, ed. (Englewood Cliffs; Prentice-Hall, Inc., 1965), p. 161.

[33] Lindeman, Edward C., *The Democratic Man* (Boston: Beacon Press, 1956), p. 208.

[34] Miller, S. M., and Rein, Martin, "Poverty and Social Change," *American Child*, Vol. XLVI No. 2 (March 1964), p. 14.

CHAPTER V

The Dysfunctional Economic System: Poverty as the Result of Economic Mismanagement

As WITH the preceding two ideal type constructs, the economic mismanagement model has two guiding assumptions: poverty in America can be eliminated through the existing social and economic institutions in our society, and this must be done primarily through an improved system of income maintenance. Advocates of this position, usually economists, frequently begin their scholarly discussions of the poverty problem by emphatic statements about the capacity of the American economy to eliminate poverty which are followed by questions about the nation's political interest in doing so. Below are listed several comments along this line. In each case the authors relate the termination of the poverty problem to some predetermined poverty line (most often, this line is the figure set by the Social Security Administration):[1]

. . . the estimates show that it is quite within the bounds of possibility for poverty to be abolished in the United States within the foreseeable future. The major problem (and it is a difficult one) is to devise means by which low-income families could be brought up to minimum standards without destroying work incentives or handicapping the operations of the economy.[2]

The United States has arrived at the point where poverty could be abolished easily and simply by the stroke of a pen. To raise every individual and family in the nation now below a subsistence income to the subsistence level would cost about $10 billion a year.[3]

Having established the capacity to eliminate poverty, the advocates of this model suggest that the primary goal is development of an adequate system of income maintenance. As they discuss this prerequisite to financial security, they point out its advantages over the service strategy discussed in Chapter 3 in relation to the culture of poverty ideal type. As various supporters of this position are quoted below, the reader should recall that each author sees the elimination of poverty as an immediate possibility in America. A sampling of the position includes the following:

It must also be said that of all the ways to assist the unfortunate, simple transfer of funds is the simplest, the least niggling, and the most respectful of human dignity. Either of two magnificently efficient agencies, the Internal Revenue Service or the Social Security Administration, can handle the affair with infinitely less sweat than the assembled social workers and Welfare Departments of the land who spend substantially smaller sums. No wonder then that economists of very different ideological preferences and diverging motives have come to perceive merit in some version or other of income maintenance as a part or (on occasion) the whole of the assault upon poverty.[4]

. . . nonetheless the stark fact remains that there is only one universal characteristic of all the poor: they do not have enough income to buy the food, clothing, shelter, medical care, and so on, that they need. So, whatever the analysis as to the causes of their poverty may be, real or tendentious, actual or spurious, they will remain poor until they have enough income not to be poor.[5]

Concern over the growing visibility of the poor and the circumstances in which many Americans were forced to live led to the creation of a national task force to investigate the problem of our nation's economically dependent population. Their report, *The Report of the President's Commission on Income Maintenance Programs,* can serve as the paradigm for the economic mismanagement ideal type. These three paragraphs from the *Report* outline the stance taken by those scholars who make up the component parts of this model in relation to each of the five dimensions of the ideal type.

We have concluded that more often than not the reason for poverty is not some personal failing, but the accident of being born to the wrong parents, or the lack of opportuniy to become unpoor, or some other circumstance over which individuals have no control.

In addition to the current poor, we have been concerned with others who easily could become poor. Most persons who depend on earnings for their incomes face the risk of losing that access to prosperity through accident, disability, loss of a breadwinner, or obsolescence of skills. Few Americans are wholly free from the economic vicissitudes of life.

We have found that existing governmental mechanisms and institutions are simply inadequate for alleviating existing poverty and protecting the nonpoor against risks that they are incapable of dealing with themselves. We have found that there is no overall system of economic security. But the Commission feels strongly that the problem of poverty must be dealt with by the Federal Government. It is possible to assure basic economic security for all Americans within the framework of existing political and economic institutions. It is time to construct a system which will provide that security.[6]

The development of an adequate income maintenance program, together with the frequently suggested supplementary services, appears to depend upon continued growth and expansion of the American economy. Those who advocate this explanatory system unanimously agree that expansion is a prerequisite to the accomplishment of any of the goals or programs which they prescribe. The elimination of poverty through some income maintenance program is actually part of a context which assumes such expansion. Gunnar Myrdal expressed this condition or contingency in saying,

It should be stressed . . . that a primary condition for success (of the War on Poverty) is rapid and steady economic expansion of the national income. Without increased demand for labor, no efforts for training and retraining workers on a mass scale can succeed. This is the important argument for the view that expanding the economy is the essential thing. Expansion is, in a sense, the necessary condition for any effort to readjust the supply of different types of labor to demand.[7]

Prior to detailed description of this ideal type along the five dimensions of the model, it is necessary to mention that the second dimension, concerned primarily with behavior traits and imputed value orientations of the lower class, is not pertinent to this ideal type. The authors whose work has been aggregated into this composite construct are not primarily interested in behavioral characteristics, life styles, or measurements of attitudes. The position of the ideal type in regard to the second dimension will therefore deal with the aggregate characteristics of those individuals who, upon empirical investigation, appear immune to general economic growth. The third dimension of the ideal type, concerning the existence of a "cycle of poverty," also does not command the attention of this explanatory framework; we shall not consider this dimension at great length.

I. *An economically deprived lower class results from structural unemployment, inadequate income maintenance programs, and low levels of productivity.*

The combination of advancing automation and insufficient governmental stimulation of the economy has created chronic unemployment among large numbers of Americans, many of whom were previously in the work force. The threat of technological advance is economic insecurity for large numbers of our population, so long as political advance is not parallel to the needs of the economically displaced. Data to support the belief that structural unemployment is a major factor in creating poverty can be drawn from comparison of prime economic growth years with those of less economic dynamism. The effect of economic expansion on low income families and individuals can be seen by dividing the fifteen year span between 1948–1963 into categories of strong expansion (1950, 1951, 1953, 1955, 1959, 1962), slow expansion (1952, 1956, 1960, 1963), and no expansion (1949, 1954, 1957, 1958, 1961) in order to examine the poverty levels during each grouping of years. In undertaking an analysis of this type, using the $3,000 family income as a measure, Weisbrod found

that in years of strong expansion, the numbers of poor families declined by an average of 667,000 per year; in the slow-expansion years the decline was a third less: 425,000 families per year; and in the no-expansion years of downturn or recession, the number of poor families rose by 400,000 per year. Thus, the difference between strong expansion and recession has been more than a million families (from a decrease of 667,000 to an increase of 425,000) among the poor. Similar effects are seen in the number of cases requiring general assistance: in the years of greatest expansion welfare rolls were cut by an average of only 5,000 cases in the slow-expansion years, and were increased by 71,000 in the years of recession.[8]

Given the increased role of the Federal Government in stimulating the national economy, some of the effects of slack years in economic growth must be attributed to macro-level mismanagement of the economy.

Given too, the structural nature of much unemployment, the programs developed to supplement the workers' incomes have been inadequate. The President's Commission on Income Maintenance Programs studied intensively the existing programs available to supplement inadequate levels of income, and concluded that major flaws existed:

Largely because of the assumption that everyone who is employable could work at adequate wages, no Federal income transfer programs have been enacted to supplement the earnings of the employed poor. Yet, one-third of all persons in poor families in 1966 lived in families headed by full-time employed male workers.[9]

Despite attempts to replace a higher proportion of earnings for lower-income workers, . . . social insurance programs still do not provide adequate benefits to the poorest. They pay adequate benefits only to those with strong labor force attachments and relatively high earnings records . . . Low wage earners will receive low social insurance benefits; thus the poor worker becomes the poor beneficiary.[10]

Other critics of the present income maintenance programs are particularly dismayed by the inadequacy of unemployment insurance programs, the bureaucratic inefficiency of public assistance, and the dependency inducing aspects of the Aid to Families with Dependent Children program.

A third and related cause of poverty, standing with structural unemployment and inadequate programs, stems from the individual's relationship to the labor force. Often, those able-bodied poor considered employable—but unemployed, and those employed either part-time or full-time but with extremely low wages, are considered to have low levels of productivity. The President's Commission addressed the question, "Why is it that employment—the basic source of income for most Americans—fails the poor?" The Commission gave the following answer,

Several factors account for this. Family size is relevant; the costs of supporting a large number of children can result in poverty for workers with even relatively high earnings. Low wages and/or lack of sufficient hours or weeks of work can account for a good deal of poverty. Disabilities prevent many from working. Poor preparation for working careers and discrimination affect many others.[11]

The Council of Economic Advisers to the President, in their 1964 *Report*, pinpoint other causes of low wages:

The chief reason for low rates of pay is low productivity, which in turn can reflect lack of education or training, physical or mental disability, or poor motivation.[12]

The advocates of the economic mismanagement position do not devote attention to the existence of distinct subcultures among the poor. Rather, they study which groups of people are poor only by the criterion of low incomes. Consequently, the second dimension of the ideal type will focus on those groups excluded from general economic development.

II. *The lower class is made up of distinct subgroups in America which can be characterized by their relative isolation from the dynamics of the national economy.*

While employed by the Joint Economic Committee of the United States Congress, Robert Lampman, an economist, worked on a study entitled *The Low Income Population and Economic Growth.* He found that some groups remained immune to national economic growth. These groups include those who were outside the labor force, those who were unable to relocate or change occupations to adapt to changes in the industrial economy, and those who belong to families headed by people sharing such "handicapping characteristics" as old age, non-white color, female sex or low education. The low income population is disproportionately (70 percent) made of individuals and families having one or more of these characteristics.[13]

The President's Commission found the groups uninfluenced by national economic trends to be those who were out of the labor force (not including the "unemployed" who are *in* the labor force), regardless of their decision in the matter: "The simple fact is that most of the poor remain poor because access to income through work is currently beyond their reach." [14]

The biological characteristics of many of those beyond the labor market can partially explain their removal; the aged, disabled, and physically or mentally ill cannot be expected to participate in the labor force, while nonwhites who are able to participate are often denied that right. The other large category of poverty stricken, female heads of households, are absent from the labor force to provide care for their young children, or because day care facilities which would allow them to work are simply not available. These groups have been labeled "high risk," which strongly indicates that they will be regularly over-represented among the low-income families. They share only their disadvantaged economic position and their isolation from the growth of the national economy.

III. *Those groups relatively isolated from general economic growth will remain poor because of inadequate income maintenance programs.*

This dimension has already been discussed above. Briefly, inter-generational poverty generally does not fall within the perspective of this type of approach to the problem of poverty. One related concern, expressed in the 1965 *Economic Report to the President* by his Council of Economic Advisers, stressed the importance of helping children escape from poverty, but little other evidence is available from the various sources used to construct this aspect of the ideal type.

IV. *To eliminate poverty, adequate income maintenance programs must be created as a first step, to be supplemented by economic policies aimed at expansion of the economy.*

As implied from the analytical stance of this ideal type, the first and most important step is the creation of an adequate income maintenance program to raise the income levels of all Americans to the poverty line. While this study is not the place to debate the various plans for such an effort, the inclusion of different forms of guaranteed annual income such as the negative income tax,[15] mothers' wages,[16] or a children's allowance,[17] are forms of such an income-based orientation to the problem of poverty. The President's Commission on Income Maintenance Programs began its series of suggested reforms in the present welfare system by stating,

Our main recommendation is for the creation of a universal income supplement program financed and administered by the Federal Government, making payments based on income needs to all members of the population. The payments would vary by family size and would produce a base income for any needy family or individual.[18]

The salience of the income-base program emerges in the second recommendation of the President's Commission:

We believe that only when the poor are assured a minimum stable income can the other mechanisms in our fight against poverty — education, training, health, and employment — begin to function adequately.[19]

This basic approach is also reflected in the concept of the relationship between an income providing program and social service programs. The Commission is absolutely clear that income is essential, social services supplementary:

The Commission feels strongly that all three types (of social services) — surrogate (represented by homemaker services or day care), informational and clinical — have to be provided as a necessary complement to an efficient and effective income maintenance system.

Services cannot be a substitute for adequate income; they cannot pay rent or buy food for a poor family. Public assistance programs frequently have offered services in lieu of adequate benefit levels.[20]

With an income maintenance program as the basis for further strategy developed out of this explanatory framework, we can now turn to other policy recommendations. Of almost equal priority to the provision of income is the continued stimulation of the economy by the Federal Government to assure increased job opportunities. Manpower programs follow from this policy position, as do efforts to recruit the low income head of a household into the labor force, to offer him training for existing jobs, and to assist him to secure employment. These programs are directed at raising the level of productivity among the lower class, and for the individual family head.

Such programs, however, must be accompanied by general economic growth stimulated by governmental policy. This relationship is captured in a statement by C. Lowell Harris to the U.S. Senate Committee on Labor and Public Welfare in 1964. Harris pointed out that many of the nation's largest employers, including the Federal Government, have few, if any jobs available to those who possess low skill levels. Harris argued that the large employers would hire these marginal people and train them on the job, if the total demands for goods and services were expanded. He concluded by referring to potential opportunities which could be enhanced by training programs financed by the government.[21] We shall discuss below possible applications of this general strategy at the community level. While these programmatic suggestions evolve from the explanatory framework, they are also extrapolations from the macro-economic level policies which form the major approach of the economic mismanagement ideal type.

V. *Changes in income maintenance policies at the national level are necessary to eliminate poverty. They must focus on continued stimulation of the economy to promote increased employment. Local derivatives of this approach will be oriented around income-producing programs.*

The program components which derive from this strategy are clear: they are oriented around producing income and/or increasing productivity levels of low-income family heads. Programs such as on-the-job training or pre-vocational skills training, intensified recruitment, and adult education related to job skills are conceptually consistent. Other programs related to increasing income might be the attempt to develop small businesses through loan programs, perhaps attached to training efforts aimed at encouraging the growth and perpetuation of small businesses. On an experimental basis, programs devoted to income guarantees or alternative forms of income maintenance would also apply.

NOTES

[1] Orshansky, Mollie, "Counting the Poor: Another Look at the Poverty Profile," *Social Security Bulletin*, Vol. XXVIII No. 1, (January 1965), is the most frequently cited resource in discussion of the poverty line.

[2] Clague, Ewan, "The Economic Context of Social Welfare in the United States," *Social Work Year Book — 1957*, (National Association of Social Workers, New York, 1957), p. 55.

[3] Morgan, James N. et al., *Income and Welfare in the United States*, (New York: McGraw-Hill, 1962).

[4] Lekachman, Robert, "Can 'More Money' End Poverty," *Poverty: Views from the Left*, Jeremy Larner and Irving Howe, eds., (New York: William Morrow & Company, Inc., 1968), pp. 58–59.

[5] Keyserling, Leon H., "The Use of Social and Economic Resources to Eliminate Poverty," *Social Welfare Forum — 1966*, (New York: Columbia University Press, 1966), p. 71.

[6] President's Commission on Income Maintenance Programs, *Poverty Amid Plenty: The American Paradox*, (November 12, 1969), pp. 1–2.

[7] Myrdal, Gunnar, "The War on Poverty," in *New Perspectives on Poverty*, Arthur B. Shostak and William Gomberg, eds., (Englewood Cliffs: Prentice-Hall, Inc., 1965), p. 126.

[8] Weisbrod, Burton A., *The Economics of Poverty: An American Paradox*, (Englewood Cliffs: Prentice-Hall, Inc., 1965), pp. 15–16.
Amid Plenty: The American Paradox, pp. 8–9.

[10] *Ibid*, pp. 14–15.

[11] *Ibid*, pp. 54–55.

[12] Council of Economic Advisers, *1964 Report to the President*, p. 66.

[13] Lampman, Robert J., "The Future of the Low-Income Problem," in Weisbrod, *The Economics of Poverty*, pp. 59–60.

[14] President's Commission on Income Maintenance Programs, *Poverty Amid Plenty: The American Paradox*, p. 49.

[15] For a discussion of the Negative Income Tax, see two articles by George H. Hildebrad: *Poverty, Income Maintenance, and the Negative Income Tax*, (Ithaca, New York: The Cornell University Press, ILR Paperback, No. 1, Reissued 1968); and "Second Thoughts on the Negative Income Tax," *Industrial Relations — A Journal of Economy and Society*, (February, 1967). See also Helen O. Nichol: "Guaranteed Income Maintenance: Negative Income Tax Plans," *Welfare in Review*, Vol. IV No. 4, (April, 1966).

[16] For a discussion of Mothers' Wages as a form of income maintenance, see: David G. Gil, "Mothers' Wages: An Alternative Attack on Poverty," *Social Work Practice — 1969*.

[17] For a discussion of Children's Allowances as a form of income maintenance, see: Scott Briar, "Why Children's Allowances?" *Social Work* (January 1969); and Irwin Garfinkel, "Negative Income Tax and Children's Allowance Programs: A Comparison," *Social Work*, (October 1968).

[18] President's Commission on Income Maintenance Programs, *Poverty Amid Plenty: The American Paradox*, p. 17.

[19] *Ibid*, p. 20.

[20] *Ibid*, p. 160.

[21] Harris, C. Lowell, "Statement on the Economic Opportunity Act of 1964," in Weisbrod, *The Economics of Poverty*, p. 116.

CHAPTER VI

The Community Action Program "Defined"

Introduction

HAVING developed three ideal type explanations for the existence of poverty, the study now turns to explore the view of this problem which emerged in the planning of the Community Action Program of the Office of Economic Opportunity. The Community Action Program (CAP) was selected for investigation in part because of the potential programmatic options available under its aegis. Other sections of the Economic Opportunity Act of 1964 clearly specified programs such as the Neighborhood Youth Corps, the Job Corps, or Volunteers in Service to America. The Community Action Program also was chosen, in part, because of the unusual configuration of organizational actors involved at the federal and local levels, because the mandated "maximum feasible participation" clause of the Act [1] stipulated the involvement of new participants in the social planning process, and because of the promise that the CAP would usher in a new style in solving our increasingly visible urban problems. A sense of the innovation in approach is apparent in the following statement from Sar Levitan, an historian of the War on Poverty:

The Economic Opportunity Act, more than any other piece of legislation, is identified with the Great Society's commitment to our nation's poor. In the typical rhetoric of the day, it was heralded as a "total war on poverty." Its announced aim was not only to eliminate poverty but to restructure society by giving the poor a chance to design and administer programs.[2]

We shall first describe the Community Action Program as part of a socio-historical setting. The next section of the chapter will discuss the Community Action Program as it emerged in conceptual form within its socio-historical context. The reader will then be able to classify the CAP with reference to the three ideal types developed earlier.

After establishing the position of the Community Action Program planners, we shall cover the structural problems of the local Community Action Agency. To understand some of the difficulties later experienced by the Community Action Agencies, we shall design a model of a local Community Action Agency based on the specifications set forth in the primary source documents used by the planners and outlined in the policy guidelines which were later published in *The Community Action Program Guide—Volume I.* In the conclusion to the chapter the conceptual explanation as defined by the Task Force will be merged with the organizational structure (the CAA), and we shall take a critical look at the internal coherence of the model developed by the Community Action Program planning group.

THE SOCIO-HISTORICAL SETTING
OF THE COMMUNITY ACTION PROGRAM

By the end of the 1950's certain undeniable facts about American society were becoming clear. Today such facts would quickly be classified as part of the urban crisis, the racial crisis, or some other category, but during this period they emerged independently of one another, almost anomalies in an otherwise affluent and complacent society. Initially, the general economic prosperity deflected concern from the manner in which the benefits of sustained economic growth were distributed. Furthermore, between 1950 and 1955 an average growth rate of about four percent annually was maintained but in the years 1955–1959 the rate declined to two and one-third percent. This drop brought with it a period of unemployment during which prices increased steadily.[3]

Identified as a problem early in the decade, unemployment grew throughout the ten-year period. As this problem attracted attention, two other related issues arose—automation and the disparity between black and white unemployment rates. The oscillation between recession and recovery that characterized the 1950's did not submerge the fact that unemployment rates continued to climb. After 1953, unemployment rose even during recovery periods as the proportion of the labor force out of work climbed from 3.5 percent in 1953 to 3.8 percent in 1956 and 5.5 percent in 1959. Special attention was drawn to rising rates of unemployment among selected groups including blacks, teenagers, blue collar workers and those with less than an eighth grade education.

The special victimization of minority group workers became clear during the 1950's. The rate of black unemployment compared to white rose from 20 percent more in 1940 to 71 percent by 1953 and 112 percent in 1963. The differentials between black and white unemployment among teenagers were even greater.

Other areas of significant disparity between racial groups appeared; foremost among them was median income. In 1949 the median income of black men was only 53 percent of the median income of white men, while black women earned 51 percent of what white women earned. The relative position of black women improved slightly, but black men fell progressively behind their white counterparts.[4] Other problems related to the employment situation and to racial concerns involved mass migration from the Deep South to the North and West, and the resultant move of the white middle class to the suburbs. City slums were once again the subject of concern, and parallels were drawn to rural depressed areas publicized in the 1954 election campaign of Paul Douglas in Illinois.

The growing visibility of social problems led to some governmental action. The 1954 amendments to the Housing Act of 1949 resulted in the creation of the urban renewal program, but neglected the citizenry most directly affected by urban renewal actions—the people coerced into relocation. Conceptual concern, as expressed in legislation, rarely led to substantive programs to aid the poor.

The air of dissatisfaction which was generated by the performance of the urban renewal program spread to other community institutions. The urban public school system came under attack, and became the central concern of the Public Affairs Division of the Ford Foundation.

The Foundation's Grey Areas Projects were focused around the expanded role of the public schools—expanded to serve the adult population of the area, pre-school youngsters, and teenagers. At approximately the same time these projects were starting, the Foundation also developed a series of experimental programs for youth and delinquent offenders. These delinquency projects came under the influence of Cloward and Ohlin's "opportunity theory," (see discussion in Chapter IV) which accounted for widespread juvenile delinquency as a reaction to a closed opportunity structure.

This breakthrough initiated by the Ford Foundation, stimulating interest in the social structure as a possible cause of problems such as delinquency or school underachievement, was followed by the Federal Government in the Juvenile Delinquency and Youth Offenses Control Act of 1961. A new administration and a new way of defining social problems had emerged.

The incorporation of the Cloward-Ohlin perspective also signaled the formal introduction of social science theory to contemporary social problems. It offered pragmatic, operational suggestions for the alleviation of delinquency and, in so doing, was capable of rational testing and evaluation. Historically, their opportunity theory played an important role in social policy formulation because it was both rationally constructed and could be applied.

The President's Committee, reflecting the Kennedy interest in the problems of youth, embraced the boldness of the Cloward and Ohlin theory. It signified the change in times, from Eisenhower to Kennedy, from wizened maturity to youth and the interest in innovation which youth symbolized. Where the Grey Areas Projects confronted stagnation in national social policy, a conservative President, and a divided Congress, the President's Committee emerged in a wave of liberal optimism and what appeared to be a call for change based on a rational, compelling challenge to the status quo.[5]

The President's Committee, according to its program coordinator, Sanford Kravitz, was committed to the Cloward and Ohlin theory, focusing on the institutions in the social structure and their role in perpetuating delinquency among lower class youth. David Hackett, a longtime friend of the Attorney General, Robert Kennedy, was brought to Washington as Executive Director of the President's Committee and head of an interagency team from HEW, the Labor Department, and the Department of Justice. According to Kravitz,

He (Hackett) had developed the concept of the program with Lloyd Ohlin, based on the Cloward and Ohlin opportunity theory. The staff was small and tightly knit for a government operation and intensely loyal to both Hackett and Ohlin. . . .

We believed that the answers to lower-class delinquency and poverty lay in a massive reform of institutional practices in schools, social-welfare agencies, and employment services. We believed with fervor that a combination of refined intellectual understanding of problems, mixed with political "clout" and new funds, would be the magic ingredients in the war on delinquency.[6]

In the programs of the President's Committee the commitment to institutional change was based on the understanding that the cause of the problem lay within the social structure. The movement toward this definition of the problem, so closely approximating the Dysfunctional Social Structure ideal type, was actively promoted by the President's Committee. Together with the Ford Foundation, the President's Committee helped develop the idea that social change was imminent, and would be focused on structural problems rather than the interests of service agencies.

It was in the programs of the Ford Foundation and the President's Committee that the concept of community action was born. Community action arose from the identification of the following problems:

1. Many voluntary "welfare" programs were not reaching the poor.
2. If they were reaching the poor, the services offered were often inappropriate.
3. Services aimed at meeting the needs of disadvantaged people were typically fragmented and unrelated.
4. Realistic understanding by professionals and community leaders of the problems faced by the poor was limited.
5. Each specialty field was typically working in encapsulated fashion on a particular kind of problem, without awareness of the other fields or of efforts toward interlock.
6. There was little political leadership involved in the decision-making of voluntary social welfare.
7. There was little or no serious participation of program beneficiaries in programs being planned and implemented by professionals and élite community leadership.[7]

In the words of one of the early community actionists, the intractability of major social institutions was also made clear. Recounting the development of the community action concept, Mitchell Sviridoff noted,

. . . the prime problem was that the established systems were rigid and unresponsive and thus failing to serve poor people as effectively as they ought. To Ylvisaker (head of the Ford Foundation's Public Affairs Department) and those working with him, this suggested "the social application of the art of jujitsu" — the process of bringing small amounts of resources to bear at points of leverage to capture larger resources otherwise working against (or ignoring) socially desirable ends. Community action, then, was not conceived as a new service concept. Services would be provided, of course, but mainly as a challenge to established institutions — a spur to social reform.[8]

Parallel to these developments, the President's Council of Economic Advisers (CEA), and particularly its chairman, Walter Heller, were becoming concerned about the growing unemployment problem, the inadequacy of existing welfare programs, and the increased hostility displayed in the cities to urban renewal. According to Arthur Schlesinger, Jr., by the spring of 1963, President Kennedy also was convinced that a broad based and comprehensive program was needed.

President Kennedy, when preparing the forthcoming legislative program for 1964, is said to have been influenced by Heller, who presented him with a study conducted by the CEA staff discussing income statistics and the continued removal of certain groups from the economy despite economic growth.[9] By the fall of 1963, just prior to the Dallas trip, Kennedy reportedly set his staff to work developing what Theodore Sorenson has called "a comprehensive, coordinated attack on poverty."

Inside and outside of the Federal Government a great deal of consideration was given to the same societal problems, and apparently from the same social structural perspective. The Ford Foundation, Mobilization for Youth, the President's Committee, and even the Council of Economic Advisers, were beginning to sharpen their focus and to concentrate on poverty as a public issue. Before the assassination, Heller began to circulate the information to officials in the government and to solicit program proposals. According to Sundquist, officials from the CEA, the Bureau of the Budget (BOB), and the White House staff were at work on this very matter when informed of the death of President Kennedy. Their program received immediate and sustaining interest from Lyndon Johnson. In his first meeting with Heller on November 23, Johnson said, "That's my kind of program. . . Move full speed ahead." [10]

The momentum was not lost after the assassination and a group of men from the executive staff, consisting of CEA and BOB upper echelon members, began to develop a planning task force which would include the dominant actors from the relatively newly developed but already "experienced" President's Committee and the Ford Foundation.

THE PLANNING PROCESS—
THE SELECTION OF A CONCEPTUAL MODEL

In recounting the development of the various programs which emerged under separate titles in the Economic Opportunity Act of 1964, James L. Sundquist credits David Hackett and Richard Boone, both from the President's Committee, with the origination and inclusion of the community action concept as part of the nascent war on poverty. They were able to convince William B. Cannon, a key staff member from the Bureau of the Budget, that community action could be the theme to highlight the new legislation. Sundquist captures the furious pace of events in Washington in his description of the incorporation of a new and as yet unclear concept into social policy:

In the course of a single week, in mid-December, aid to community organizations was transformed from an incidental idea in the War on Poverty into the entire war. The Budget Bureau staff first assigned for the purpose $100 million of the $500 million that had been set aside in the budget to finance the anti-poverty legislation, but a few days later they had committed the whole amount. Schultze (the Assistant Budget Director) had endorsed the idea to Budget Director Kermit Gordon, with a note that a better name than "development corporation" (the original name for a community action agency, suggested by Cannon) was needed. The phrase "action program" was found buried in Cannon's original memorandum; somebody put the word "community" in front, and the name was born.[11]

The acknowledged proponents of the community action concept—Paul Ylvisaker of the Ford Foundation, the administrators of local Grey Area Projects and project directors from funded programs of the President's Committee—were brought in to reinforce the concept for Gordon. Later, together with Heller, the Budget Director approached the President and succeeded in getting his approval to incorporate the idea into the War on Poverty.

As part of developing the new legislation, several task forces were created to work out the detailed arrangements which would be presented to the Congress. The Task Force on Urban Areas was assigned the job of delineating the legislative specifications and attendant administrative regulations which would emerge as the Community Action Program. The men assigned to coordinate the Task Force were Sanford Kravitz of the President's Committee and Frederick Hayes from the Urban Renewal Administration. The Task Force had to apply an undefined concept. While creating this formulation, it had to rely upon the few people who could claim any knowledge or experience with community action. The planning group which constituted the Task Force, drawing on both governmental and private sources, included key staff members from the President's Committee, local Ford-funded and delinquency projects, and several "outsiders" known to be sympathetic to their views. In describing the Task Force, John Donovan notes, ". . . by and large, Federal expertise was limited to members of the Juvenile Delinquency Committee staff."[12]

Given the control of the Task Force, the staff members from the President's Committee could be expected to exercise substantial influence in determining the perception of the problem to be addressed by community action. In the deliberations of the Task Force, the conceptual framework of the President's Committee together with that of the Ford Foundation in its Grey Area Projects and delinquency programs would obviously dominate. The incorporation of their conceptual stances, so heavily dependent upon the opportunity theory of Cloward and Ohlin, will be pursued below.

In discussing the social action strategies of the Ford Foundation and the President's Committee, we can distinguish several differences. These differences lie more in the structure and function of the implementing agency at the local level, however, than in the approach to the problem:

Both placed the emphasis upon changing the environment, rather than the individual, and both recognized education and vocational opportunities as crucial aspects of the environment. Reform, they both believed, must grow out of a much more coherent integration of relevant institutions.[13]

The accounts of the planning process refer time after time to the social structural causation of problems. This position is attributed to the planners of the national community action program by Donovan, Wofford, Sundquist, Kravitz, Grossman, and Marris and Rein. Each of these authors depicts the institutional change orientation of the planning group, and in so doing, implies the structural causation explanatory framework of the Dysfunctional Social System ideal type. The affinity of the planners with the social structural position is particularly explicit in relation to their attacks on ineffective social institutions, in their insistence upon opening up opportunities to the poor, and in their support for increasing the power of the poor over the institutions which affect their lives.

The members of the Task Force on Urban Areas clearly

were conscious of the powerlessness of the poor before the
service and political institutions of the community. The planners intended to provide some measure of shared power in
planning and policy-making. Donovan reflects this interpretation by saying, "In community action the revolutionary aspects
of the war on poverty came to a focus; power was to be given
to those not included in any establishment."[14] The planners'
intentions were embodied in the "maximum feasible participation" clause of the legislation which mandated the involvement
of the poor in the policy and planning process of the local level.

Donovan delineates the meaning of community action conceptually, noting explicitly its attack on the institutions of the
society:

Community action was fervently anti-establishment; schools, employment services, welfare agencies, city hall were all part of an
"establishment" or "system" which served "the disadvantaged" by
referring them from one "helping service" to another without ever
really understanding or challenging "the culture of poverty" and
with no real ability to move families out of poverty.[15]

While perhaps overstretching the radicalism of the challenges to the legitimacy of the existing institutions, Donovan
captures the flavor of the concept and the planners' notion of
what form participation would take.

John Wofford, who came to the Community Action Program
from a position as staff member of the President's Task Force
on the War Against Poverty, also discussed the structural
change orientation of the planners. Maximum feasible participation was defined by Wofford and his colleagues as an
attempt to ameliorate the conditions of powerlessness. This
condition was defined to mean that the poor had little power
to affect their own environment; numerous decisions of direct
relevance to their lives were made by removed, unconcerned
bureaucracies, absentee landlords, greed-ridden businessmen,

and agents of City Hall such as the police. This condition of powerlessness would be altered by giving the poor some authority through participation in the planning and administration of programs designed to serve them. The staff of the Community Action Program, from its inception in August, 1964, concerned itself with this aspect of the program in reviewing program proposals.[16]

Marris and Rein traced the maximum feasible participation concept back to the President's Committee and the Ford Foundation programs. Based on the planners' skepticism about the capacity of existing institutions to voluntarily provide meaningful programs for the poor, the logical role for the poor was to participate in the planning supposed to benefit them. Mistrust of traditional planning organizations brought about the inclusion of the poor in the new agencies set up to develop and conduct delinquency programs. This principle of inclusion was carried over to the community action program. Besides insuring a voice in decisions, participation would guarantee distribution of employment opportunities:

Participation was thus to restore dignity, redistribute power, and ensure that, wherever possible, the poor themselves were recruited for the jobs that the programs would create.[17]

Kravitz supports this contention, noting that while the creation of new subprofessional employment opportunities was emphasized by the planners;

During this period there was clearly a concern for the presence of residents at the neighborhood advisory-board level, but the question of resident control of community-action agencies never arose and was never cited as a basic requirement by those of us who were planning the program. The clear intent was to substantially increase resident participation in program development and in the administration of programs at the neighborhood level.[18]

Whether the degree of resident participation in planning and policy-making in the new community action programs would amount to control or substantial influence is a moot point. Unfortunately, various critics as well as advocates of the practice have created a literature on this issue without regard to determining the impact, if any, of such participation. From a review of the literature, giving particular credence to the accounts of the planning process written by members of the Task Force, the phrase in the legislation requiring "maximum feasible participation of residents of the areas and members of the groups served," was drawn from a social structural explanation of the problem and designed to increase the power of the poor vis-a-vis the institutions of the social order.

The planning group on the Task Force on Urban Areas was given case material to use in applying further the community action concept. Remember that a name—"community action program"—was created without a program, while several existing programs funded by the President's Committee and the Ford Foundation were promoted as paradigms of community action strategy. This complementarity, in addition to the staffing pattern of the Task Force, led to the adoption of Ford and President's Committee projects as models for the forthcoming community action agencies.

The planners were given brief descriptions of several such programs to examine (four of these verbatim records are included below). As one reads these illustrations he should remember that they were perceived by Task Force members as part of a conceptual framework which derived from opportunity theory, and all programs were constructed around a strategy of institutional change through social action. We refer the reader to the four brief case studies for understanding how commitment to the social structural model—which went unchallenged on the Task Force [19]—restricted the participants to this perspective.

Case 1

NEW YORK CITY[20]

Mobilization for Youth

Four neighborhood service centers are providing a variety of rapid services in an informal manner to meet the problems of residents of New York's Lower East Side. An integral part of the Mobilization for Youth project, these centers act as intermediaries between local families and such institutions as the School, the Housing Authority, the Welfare Department and the Police, complex bureaucracies with which many feel powerless to cope.

Open seven days a week, daytime and evenings, the centers, scattered throughout the Lower East Side area, served over 5,000 individuals during their first year of service. Center staff have dealt with problems ranging from emotional distress to obtaining college scholarships, from assisting newly released youthful offenders to the vocational guidance, job training and placement of drug addicts. Fifteen visiting homemakers, local women hired and trained by Mobilization, receive requests from service centers to help neghborhood women to learn to cook with surplus foods, care for their children, find a doctor, or refurbish furniture.

A consumers aid clinic in one center teaches residents about installment buying, credit, comparative shopping and helps solve individual problems of low-income consumers.

These centers work with existing public and private agencies for the benefit of those in need — those who all too often are overlooked or who fall between the cracks of traditional services. About half of the youths and adults simply walk in to the centers; the other are referred by the Welfare Department, the City Housing Authority, the Police, the schools, the Lower East Side Neighborhood Association and other Mobilization programs. The centers, in turn, work with the appropriate agencies. For example, a visiting homemaker referred the unemployed husband of one woman to Mobilization's Urban Work Corps where he now has a job as a carpenter. One family's apartment was overrun with rats. A staff member in the neighboring service center contacted the appropriate official in the Housing Authority and notified the Welfare Department. In helping released delinquents, the centers work with state correctional schools and voluntary agencies. The job placement program for addicts is conducted with the help of the Lower East Side Narcotics Information service and Mobilization work projects.

Education

A Homework Helper program is paying 300 outstanding high school students from low-income families to tutor 1,000 grade school students who are failing in their studies.

A Curriculum Planning Program is developing text material more closely related to the real lives of low-income and minority groups.

Other education programs include reading centers and remedial reading clinics in elementary schools and expanded guidance in elementary and junior high schools. One junior high school program will bring in community adults who have been successful in various occupations to discuss career possibilities with students.

Home visits by teachers are underway as part of a School-Community Relations course, providing teachers with better understanding of their pupils' cultural backgrounds and problems.

Employment

The Youth Jobs Center serves as a central employment agency to place youngsters in jobs in the regular labor market or in Mobilization's subsidized work programs.

The Urban Service Corps, a subsidized work program, provides basic skills and training in work habits for out-of-school, out-of-work youths from 16 to 21. Projects include work in a Mobilization-owned luncheonette, repairing the roof of an area settlement house and serving as aides in a public hospital.

Recreation

Three coffee shops serve as social and cultural storefront centers symbolic of the style and mood of neighborhood youth. Delinquent and potential delinquent youngsters operate the shops under informal supervision.

The Adventure Corps offers boys aged 9 to 13 a variety of recreational, educational, cultural and vocational activities. Divided into squads, the Corps is organized through existing settlement houses and agencies in the area.

Community Organization

Community organizers are strengthening existing neighborhood council (sic) and making new attempts to organize the unaffiliated. Storefront churches, hometown clubs, Negro and Puerto Rican organizations are participating in this effort.

Legal

A legal services program is assisting the poor people in the target area to obtain equal justice and competent legal aid. The program is concerned with legal programs relating to narcotics addiction, housing, unemployment insurance, consumers' aid, social welfare and criminal violations. Mobilization is the third organization in the history of New York City to be granted the right by the courts to engage in legal aid assistance.

Case 2

COMMUNITY PROGRESS, INC. NEW HAVEN[21]

The preventive and restorative programs carried on in the six inner neighborhoods in New Haven are coordinated and linked together by the Neighborhood Services Division. This Division is made up of a Neighborhood Services Coordinator, a Community School Coordinator, and Neighborhood Workers, who are indigenous to each neighborhood. These offices are located in the Community School and in the Employment Centers. This Division provides the linkages necessary to bring together the variety of on-going programs under CPI direction.

The staff of the neighborhood Services Team provides insight into the life and problems of the local community. They encourage parents' participation in school, marshal services to support youth and their families in employment programs; provide referral to legal aid services, adult education, health clinics, civic, recreational, cultural, and athletic programs; and organize discussions and planning groups to attack the problems of the neighborhood.

For the *Education Program*, they operate the recreational programs, refer to family services youth and families recommended by the school, interpret and support the schools' program to the parents. The Community Schools, using Neighborhood staff, are the base for neighborhood organization and social services.

For the *Leisure Time Program,* they provide leadership in planning and carrying out leisure time activities in the Community Schools. They involve public agencies, such as Parks and Recreation, and group work agencies in these programs. They provide staff for some programs, auxiliary staff for others. Local community groups, including youth, are brought together to plan leisure time programs, raise funds, and allot funds made available through public agencies. There had been no previous links of the leisure time program to any of the other systems. Contacts through the leisure time program are coordinated with other services for youth and families, in employment, education, law, corrections, and welfare.

For the *Employment Program,* the Neighborhood workers are located in the Employment Center to recruit youths for the employment programs, and to provide supportive services for trainees and those i early stages of employment. They provide essential conjunctive services in health, family service, welfare, and others as they are needed by the trainees and their families.

For the *Law-Correctional Program,* they work with police, probation and parole officers to develop tailor-made individual plans for juvenile delinquents and youthful offenders. They provide a coalition of leisure time, educational, employment, family service and direct personal assistance where it is needed to improve rehabilitation services. They make referrals to the Neighborhood Legal services.

For the *Health and Welfare Program,* the Neighborhood Coordinator will have the major responsibility of integrating family welfare programs at the neighborhood level. They will be a major referral source to new Community Health Services and will integrate these services with other health services available in the neighborhood. They will highlight gaps in community services, which will develop during their case finding. They will interpret new welfare projects and will provide the essential linkages to law and correctional programs, leisure time and educational systems. This should provide the maximum use of available services through better coordination at the local level. They enlist local families to participate in housing programs.

The Neighborhood Service Team will provide the staff service and major thrust in developing the *Community organization activities* essential to a community development program.

Case 3

NEW YORK CITY CENTRAL HARLEM[22]

Harlem Youth Unlimited: A new youth movement

In Central Harlem, as part of HARYOU's demonstration program, an independently incorporated youth movement will be formed — Harlem Youth Unlimited. This massive new youth movement promises to create a new youth culture to replace the culture of apathy and alienation which exists.

This new program is a natural outgrowth of HARYOU's planning period, in which a group of "HARYOU Associates" played a crucial role, gathering data, conducting a survey among the youth, developing pilot projects such as a coffee shop, a company of performers, participating in social action (including a massive youth rally in City Hall in support of the Federal youth program, participation in the March on Washington, the voter registration drive, the activities of the Community Council on Housing), and contributing in many other ways to the planning process.

Now the new Harlem Youth Unlimited will develop an enlarged program, building on its earlier activities, establishing a new Business Enterprise system and developing new social action.

By itself HYU would be just another group, with the minimal impact of previous youth groups. As an integral part of the total comprehensive program for Central Harlem, HYU has an opportunity to be much more. HYU will be involved responsibly in every piece of the HARYOU program.

It will provide youth leadership to occupy one-third of the places on HARYOU's neighborhood boards, which will guide the policies and programs of HARYOU.

Through some 250 youth block captains it will be a major part of HARYOU's social action and community information program.

Specific paid jobs have already been designated for 1400 HYU youth in HARYOU's junior academies as group work aides, in the senior academies as discussion leaders, as officers in HARYOU's cadet corps, as helpers in the pre-school program, as aides in the health services program, etc.

HYU members will work with adult researchers in data gathering and analysis.

HYU's coffee shops will provide recreation programs for youth participating in many of HARYOU's programs.

HYU's Business Enterprises will service many of HARYOU's office, public relations, and construction needs.

HARYOU's Community Action Institute will train HYU members for their positions of leadership in community action and community service.

HARYOU's youth training and employment program will utilize HYU's Business Enterprises program for on-the-job training.

Talented members of HARYOU's Arts and Culture classes will form the nucleus of HYU's performing companies.

In these ways and in many others, this unique youth movement will feed into the basic services of HARYOU's comprehensive program, and will, in turn, be enriched by it.

Education

Re-structuring of Public Schools — In close cooperation with the Superintendent of Schools, a drastic overhaul of all schools in Central Harlem, including reorganization of classes, revised curriculum, new materials, outstanding teachers and appropriate incentives. Transition to new school program to be provided through Reading Mobilization Year, in which all 4–8 grades would eliminate other activities to focus on improving reading.

Pre-school Academies — To provide 4,000 nursery age children with pre-school education and to work closely with their parents. Local mothers will play important role — as teachers, assistants, etc.

After-school Remediation — To raise reading achievement level of young people who have fallen behind. Program to be operated by Harlem Teachers Association through numerous after-school centers or churches, storefronts, and other community facilities, utilizing advanced techniques, small teacher-pupil ratios, programmed instruction methods, etc.

Youth Employment Program

Under HARYOU other Harlem agencies to operate five employment centers will provide full battery of services required to make Harlem youth employable. Continuing counseling and guidance will be available. Youth not ready to be trained for specific occupations will receive remedial education and/or will participate in exploratory work programs through a Community Service Corps. Skill training will be offered in on-the-job situations, apprenticeships, and classes. Special staff will be assigned to work with employers to develop job opportunities and place young people on jobs.

Junior and Senior Academies

Halfway houses which will provide a transition between the institution and return to the community, with focus on remediation and learning basic educational and work skills.

Institute for Narcotics Research

Detoxification, counseling, group therapy programs for drug users. Concomitant community action program to bring to public attention, and eradicate illegal drug traffic in Central Harlem.

Cadet Corps

A recreation program for pre-teens, building an espirit de corps through uniformed units sponsored by churches and community groups. Remediation tied into program, and advancement through the ranks tied to achievement in studies.

Clinical and Family Services

Through the Inter-Departmental Neighborhood Centers of New York.

Arts and Cultural Programs

Sculpture, art, music, drama, etc.

Community Action Institute

Training for all youth, lay people and professionals who participate in comprehensive program.

Neighborhood Boards

Youth and adults on five local boards overseeing policy and program within their neighborhoods. Programs of health services, social action, research and information services.

Harlem Youth Unlimited

An independent mass youth movement cooperating in all areas of HARYOU demonstration and building new youth cultures through programs including community action, coffee shop cultural centers, performing companies and business enterprises.

Case 4

LANE COUNTY, OREGON[23]

Community Youth Worker Program

The Lane County Youth Study Board which is launching a comprehensive demonstration program, will provide as one element in this program the services of Community Youth Workers. The Community Youth Worker will serve as the rural counterpart of the "urban detached worker." Although there is little gang activity in Lane County in the sense that there is in major urban centers, problem youth in rural areas do congregate in trouble spots where they become involved in delinquent activities. Further, youth in rural areas are dispersed, and consequently, "invisible," unable to be reached by community agencies, and frequently falling between the cracks in agency services.

The Lane County Youth Study Board will send out Community Youth Workers who will locate and engage young people in the hinterlands. They will attempt to direct them toward positive behavior and to link them with community resources which can assist them.

A frequent problem with prior detached worker programs has been their focus on particular groups of youngsters without an effective linkage to appropriate community resources. As part of an integrated program, the Community Youth Workers' ability to help young people will be improved considerably.

The Community Youth Worker

The Community Youth Worker will feed young people into the Youth Study Board training and employment program which will provide continuing counseling, remedial education, work skills training, job placement and job development.

The Youth Study Board will set up special youth group programs through the YMCA and YWCA which will be designed especially to serve youngsters recruited by Community Youth Workers.

The Lane County school district and its subsidiary systems within Eugene, Junction City, and Oakridge are deeply involved in the Youth Study Board's demonstration program; Community Youth Workers will work with school dropouts toward returning them to school, where appropriate, to take advantage of new school programs being developed, such as the half-day school — half-day work program or the proposed new vocational skills training center.

The Community Youth Worker will serve as a case finder for a new program of service to hard-core families being developed by the Youth Study Board in coordination with the Family Service Agency, the Public Welfare Department and the Juvenile Department.

The Community Service Worker

Concomitantly, the Youth Study Board will have Community Service Workers who will reach out to adults in the hinterland, developing community planning committees of local residents, operating leadership training programs and providing many new vehicles for citizen participation. The Community Service Workers and the Youth Workers will operate as a team, linking their activities to bring "invisible" youth and adults together into meaningful participation in community life.

The Youth Study Board works closely with all pertinent community agencies, and is establishing a new Agency Planning and Development Committee. Through the efforts of the reaching-out workers, the voices of young people and adults will now be heard as agencies develop their services.

Community Youth Workers will also develop opportunities for young people directly in community service such as the new program of volunteer participation in the probation services of the Juvenile Department, which is a part of the comprehensive program.

Education

Curriculum Planning and Development Committees — composed of teachers, parents, and youth of Eugene, Oakridge and Junction City.

To develop curriculum changes for elementary, junior and senior high schools.

Curriculum and Methods Development Center — a repository for the latest innovations in education materials and techniques, and a resource to all local school personnel.

Work Orientation Programs — one semester orientation to World-of-Work for ninth graders.

Skill Orientation Program — year-long classes for high school students, introducing them to variety of skills.

Work Experience — half-day school, half-day work program for high school students.

Early Enrichment Program — enrichment of total elementary school program through trips, cultural activities, community experiences, etc.

Special Group Resources Program — Higher Horizon type program for secondary schools.

Tutoring — after school for all grade levels, using older students to tutor younger ones.

New Testing, Counseling, and Guidance Programs

Teacher Training Programs

Employment

Youth Opportunities Centers — providing identification and recruitment of unemployed, out-of school youth (frequently "invisible" in rural areas); testing, counseling, guidance for all youth. Remedial education and work orientation for youngsters not ready for skills training. Skills training in MDTA classes, on-the-job training and apprenticeships. Job placement services. Special work with industry, business, and labor, to develop job opportunities for youth, including a Business, Industry, Labor, and Education Committee. Feedback of latest labor market material into school vocational program.

Special vocational rehabilitation program for youngsters with physical and/or mental handicaps.

Agency Programs

Agency Planning and Development Committee — a new organization providing continuing coordination and planning for public and private agencies.

Cooperative Agency Service Effort (*CASE*) — special service program for multi-problem families, coordinating family service agency, Public Welfare Department, and Juvenile Department.

Information Centers — to be established in rural areas, where knowledge of community services is limited.

Juvenile Department Volunteer Program — developing new approaches to using volunteers in probation services.

YM-YWCA Special Group Programs — experimental group programs for previously unreached male teenagers and female dropouts.

Community Development

This program would be operated in conjunction with the Federal Extension Service of USDA. It would include:

Community Service Coordinators who would reach out into the hinterlands developing *Community Planning Committees* to give people in rural areas an opportunity to plan for their own needs; *Citizen Participation Programs,* and *Leadership Development and Training Programs.*

Community Youth Workers — the rural counterpart of the urban "detached worker." Reaches out to young people in the hinterlands to connect them with community resources and involves them in constructive participation in community life. Works as a team with Community Service Coordinators, and links youth with all programs of Youth Study Board.

A careful examination of these four project summaries, when free from a context imbued with opportunity theory and its related orientation to institutional change, indicates that a sub-

stantial majority of these programs were traditional social services, expansions of these services, remedial education, or other
activities which were not related to increasing the power of
the poor, directly changing institutions, or opening opportunity
structures. To be sure, elements of these latter strategies
appear, but the important point is that the entire program for
each of the communities involved was conceived by the Task
Force members as consistent with their social action orientation. The social service, compensatory education and vocational counseling programs were justified by the planners as
strategically required inducements to social reform which
were seen as prerequisites to the transformation of local institutions. This perspective continued to allow the Task Force
members to deliberate rather than evaluate conceptually the
impact of "model" projects from the Ford Foundation or the
President's Committee on the community structures which
administered the programs. Given the astute perception and
intelligence of the planning group, what could account for this
apparent oversight?

Commitment to an accelerated course of social change, emphasized by the revolutionary social structural definition of
the poverty problem, characterized the people involved in the
Ford, President's Committee, and Task Force planning groups
and the programs which they created. The emotional zeal the
planners possessed carried with it a sense of certainty that they
were discovering solutions to the problems which plagued society. Attacks and investigations by city governments and established agencies on Mobilization for Youth and its subsequent
withdrawal from institutional change strategies; the retreat
from conflict-producing programs into social services clear in
other projects;[24] and the overt failure of the Foundation and
President's Committee projects to persuade the established
local institutions to become more responsive to the needs of
the poor[25] were all explained by the planners' perspective as
necessary steps en route to the original goal of social reform.

Their organizational strategy, which called for involvement of the traditional agencies in the community, justified the meagre innovation in program efforts despite obvious contradictions to the original goals posed by the programs funded.

The planners' commitment to the social structural explanatory framework led to the construction of a model administrative organization (for the CAA) which did not derive from their problem definition. Their problem definition also implicitly included the notion that change was politically determined and required organized pressure by potential beneficiaries. Organization of the poor, community development, and participation in the planning process were all concepts which contained this implication about the process of social change.

But the planners were employed, after all, by agencies of the federal government or the Ford Foundation. It is assumed that the sponsorship of reform by such acknowledged components of the social structure did not extend to the stimulation of revolution. Planned social change, orderly revision, scientifically controlled and tested strategies to improve a social condition could be supported, but direct attacks on the social order were not likely to be on the agendas of institutions which gained their power and authority from the existing structural arrangements within the society.

The planners were forced to reconcile these constraints despite their rhetoric, and the logical system for implementation of their plans was premised on incremental changes which would be brought about through the involvement, commitment, and reform-from-within of local institutions. The institutional constraints caused by being a part of the dysfunctional social structure made it unlikely that a revolution in fact, as opposed to a revolution in thought, would be officially promoted. The planners, who operated within these limitations, can be considered as embodiments of utopian thinkers in Mannheim's sense,

. . . intellectually so strongly interested in the destruction and transformation of a given condition of society that they unwittingly see
only those elements in the situation which tend to negate it. Their
thinking is incapable of correctly diagnosing an existing condition
of society . . . it can be used only as a direction for action.[26]

When the ideas of the planners were overruled by the actions
of the agencies, readjustment in operational strategy would
have been a more appropriate response than a reaffirmation
of the original definition of problems and goals. But the planners were intent on the implementation of their program of
social reform, settling for written acknowledgement of opportunity theory or the concept of powerlessness as these concepts
were expressed in the proposals for funds which came in from
the cities. The inaccuracy in diagnosis referred to by Mannheim was clear in the planners' expectations about the local
agencies' interest in self-renovation. The stubborn resistance
to change shown by local organizations was rationalized by
the planners' organizational strategy and the dominant position
of their conceptual framework. Mannheim depicts such anoma-
lous circumstances as characteristic of the liberal-humanitarian
form of utopian thinking:

In its characteristic form, it also establishes a "correct" rational conception to be set off against evil reality. This counter-conception is
not used, however, as a blueprint in accordance with which at any
given point in time the world is to be reconstructed. Rather it serves
merely as a "measuring rod" by means of which the course of concrete events may be theoretically evaluated. The utopia of the
liberal-humanitarian mentality is the "idea." [27]

It was this same kind of idea, in force at the period, which
allowed the Civil Rights movement to celebrate the "victories"
of legislative success and to ignore the plight of the poor black
man in the rural South and the urban North.

Before moving on to the next section which examines the
model organizational structure of the local community action

agency, the author wishes to re-emphasize that one must consider the thinking of the Task Force planners within its social and historical context. That context was the early 1960's, and the leadership and tone of the country was liberal-humanitarian. The planners of the 1960's who designed the programs of the Ford Foundation, the President's Committee, and the Community Action Program were *the* social activists, *the* avant-garde of reform of that time. As an employee of the Community Action Program, the author shared the same spirit and enthusiasm as well as the belief which allowed the rhetoric and the real to merge into a consistent explanatory framework and a radically innovative approach to solving social problems.

THE PLANNING PROCESS— THE SELECTION OF AN OPERATIONAL MODEL

For different but well rationalized reasons, both the Ford Foundation and the President's Committee chose to have their action programs developed and administered at the local community level by new (or, in the case of the President's Committee, recently created) organizations. They further specified that these local organizations coordinate the operations of powerful actors on the community stage, often including the Mayor's office, the public school system, the planning organization for the voluntary social agencies (United Community Services, or whatever its local name might be) and perhaps the public welfare agency, the urban renewal authority, the juvenile courts, or a federation of settlement houses. These agencies were all required for the attack on either the outmoded schools, delinquency, or poverty (while the object of attack changed with the times, the insistence on the structure remained the same). The inclusion of these various organizations was part of the adamant demand for comprehensive programming. These three factors—a local base, coordination, and comprehensive programming—were the standards against which local projects were presumed to be judged.

The initial emphasis on locally based organization came from the Ford Foundation's interest in the public schools. The Foundation saw potential for remaking the public school systems of the inner cities into educational and community service institutions offering the entire population a full range of educational and social programs. The Foundation instigated the development of new agencies to integrate the public and private service agencies through the development of new programs.

The Foundation held that local leadership had to be stimulated to propose and implement needed reforms. This could be accomplished by inducement, i.e., by money offered to those cities which were willing and able to marshal the required local leadership into a new coordinative body eligible for Foundation funds. The principle of reform through inducement was transferred from the new organization to its member units, who, upon participating in the new and innovative enterprise, were also to develop innovations.

Marris and Rein have summarized the guiding assumptions of the Foundation, limited as it had to be by its unique position in American society, a position of "power without responsibility,"

Poverty, unemployment and delinquency were taken as symptoms of a pervasive hardening of the social and bureaucratic structure. The first step, therefore, was to break out of this constricting framework in any promising direction. Once the institutions of the city came together, and saw the problem as a whole, once they examined their performance in the light of this understanding, once the leaders everywhere in the community committed themselves to seek authentic solutions, then the logic of this commitment would drive institutions towards experiment and cooperation.[28]

Because the problems were massive, and pervasive throughout

the community structure, the Foundation pressed for broad representation on the policy-making boards of the new organizations. This also seemed a necessary precaution to prevent domination of the new agency by any existing organization.

The President's Committee, also seeking to reform apathetic local governments and school systems, joined the Foundation in using rational persuasion as its major tactic of reform. It even went beyond the Foundation in placing extreme emphasis on rational social planning, which specified the development of a theoretical framework, required the collection of substantial information about the community, and insisted upon a readiness to engage in extensive evaluative research. Operating out of the structural change orientation, the Committee also insisted that the locally developed organization have the "authority and community influence to bring such changes about." Social reform was to be implemented through rational planning which coordinated the academic expertise with liberal political leadership. The focus of reform strategies were the vested interests and conservative practices of local service bureaucracies. The strategy for change was based upon the rational persuasiveness of the Committee's planning process, since they did not have the political "clout" to force change at the local level. The emphasis on planning, documentation, and problem analysis and evaluation was designed to offset power deficiencies with persuasive argumentation. Innovation, it was thought, could result from an altered understanding of the delinquency problem and the roles played by institutional interests.[29]

Compelled by an absence of coercive power, relatively meagre resources, and the possession of a truth (social structural theory), the staff of the Committee logically followed the same path as the Foundation. Local coordinative agencies were required to develop the "commitment" (a key term for the Committee) and thrust toward innovation, to generate the local "clout" (political power necessary to encourage reform—

another key word in the new vocabulary of planned social
change), and to spend the federal dollars.

While the Foundation emphasized community leadership
and consensus planning and the Committee stressed rational
social planning, the similarities between the two funding organizations far outweighed their differences when it came to the
question of the structure required of local agencies. A broadly
representative structure was preferred by both the Foundation
and the Committee; board members were to include major
public and private institutions as well as established financial,
political, religious and racial leaders. The local governmental
body had to participate because of its control over resources
and coordinating functions. Thus, the established power in
the community would be induced to join a new coalition
oriented to reform—and the inducement for entering such an
alliance was money. With Federal or Foundation money as
the carrot, local power could be stimulated to engage in a
planning process in which the planners would convince themselves of the need for reform and innovation based on rational
assessment of the problems and a program for change supported by all relevant constituencies.[30]

As might be expected from the continuity in personnel and
in conceptual orientation from the Ford Foundation and the
President's Committee to the Task Force on Urban Areas, the
development of the organizational model for the anti-poverty
program's local community action agency also closely approxi-
mated the models acceptable to its predecessors. Robert
Lefferts, a Task Force member, said that the CAP planning
group spent most of its time deliberating the alternative structures which the local community action agency might take.
The conceptual framework was never at issue. Other assumptions which were not questioned included those carried over
from the Foundation and Committee experiences—the focus
of community action would be the locality, the structure would
incorporate established service systems (both to marshal the

required "clout," and to develop the "involvement" which led to organizational self-renovation), and the program would be comprehensive in scope. According to Lefferts, the Task Force projected the following process: Agencies and other powerful actors would be brought together and "involved" in the structure of the local community action agency; as they became involved, they would develop "clout"; institutional change, the main objective of the community action program, would derive from involved powerful agencies, committed to reform and persuaded to change by the clout of the community action agency.[31]

The recollections of Sanford Kravitz, the coordinator of the Task Force, are consistent with those above:

Our model of how the community-action program would work went something like this: A community would carefully study its poverty problems, locate the most severe pockets of need, and identify them as target areas slated for intensive effort. It would plan a program for these areas that would affect all relevant institutions, that is, the schools, social services, job opportunities. It would enhance its ability to implement its program objectives by inclusion of political leadership. It would "remain honest" to its purposes by inclusion of voices representing the poor, residents of the target neighborhoods. Thus, the model implied a central local authority to exert influence on and make decisions about the local poverty program, presumed the capacity to engage the major community-service-delivery institutions in a coordinated effort, and above all, assumed the power of persuasion necessary to allocate resources to carry on the program.[32]

This representation of the planners' position clearly illustrates the relationship between the community action program and its conceptual benefactors. The specific entities inherited—a local base, coordination, and comprehensiveness—are designated in the *Preliminary Report* of the Task Force.

Throughout the *Report* no other geographic referent for community action is mentioned aside from "the community." Under the title, "The Goals of a Community Action Program," the *Report* declares,

A CAP provides a means whereby a community can look *anew* and *comprehensively* at the problem of poverty. It enables the various local agencies and citizens to plan *together,* and from their pooled experiences and diverse perspectives, to find new and more effective ways to reduce poverty. This major goal is different and far more challenging than merely providing money to the various participating agencies to enable them to improve their services.[33] (Emphasis is from the original source.)

Four major goals are specified in the *Report:* Coordination and Development of Services, Involvement of the People in Need of Help, Stimulation of Change, and Mobilization of the Community. Under the heading, "General Criteria," the *Report* first establishes that

A Community Action Organization should represent the key groups at interest in the community. Government, Public and Private Service Agencies, Business, Labor, Civic, Cause or Action-Oriented Groups(e.g., Urban League, NAACP, League of Women Voters), Neighborhood organizations of low-income persons, Racial or Ethnic group representatives.[34]

Coordination of the governmental authority and its public agencies with the "key service agencies" is specified, with both intended as participants in the policy-making and program development of the community action organization.

In addition to the policy-making role, the involvement of existing organizations is expanded to include their participation as administrators of programs. The section of the *Report* entitled "Structure" states,

Ordinarily, a Community Action Organization will utilize the appropriate community agencies for the mounting of anti-poverty programs, e.g., public schools, visiting nurse services, employment services, public and private welfare agencies, etc. This is usually preferable to program operation by the Community Action Organization itself.[35]

While varying structures could be devised consistent with

these goals, the locally constructed community action organization had to meet the criteria discussed above, and to provide for participation of those intended as program beneficiaries. The concluding section of this chapter will present the actual model developed and several questions about the model which the utopianism of the Task Force planners overlooked.

THE COMMUNITY ACTION AGENCY MODEL

The input of the Task Force on the final model selected for the Community Action Program is apparent in the anti-poverty legislation, the Economic Opportunity Act of 1964, and in the administrative regulations published by the newly formed Office of Economic Opportunity to inform local communities of the Community Action Program. These regulations or guidelines, found in the *Community Action Program Guide* (Volume I), detail the intent of the Act and clarify issues raised in the legislation. To develop the model which evolved from the planning process, both the legislation and the *Guide* will be used.

The first carry-over from the Task Force, and from the Committee, was the use of language reminiscent of opportunity theory. It appears most significantly in the initial statement of the Act under "Findings and Declaration of Purpose":

The United States can achieve its full economic and social potential as a nation only if every individual has the opportunity to contribute to the full extent of his capabilities and to participate in the workings of our society. It is therefore, the policy of the United States to eliminate the paradox of poverty in the midst of plenty in this Nation by opening to everyone the opportunity for education and training, the opportunity to work, and the opportunity to live in decency and dignity. It is the purpose of this Act to strengthen, supplement, and coordinate efforts in the furtherance of that policy.[36]

Title II-A of the Act, concerning Community Action Programs, specifies what a Community Action Program is and what it should undertake. As the legislation implies, concepts rationalized by the planners to remain compatible with the social structural approach (generally focused on individual change strategies) were given a substantial role. Section 202 establishes that a "community action program" is one—

(1) which mobilizes and utilizes resources, public or private, of any urban or rural, or combined urban and rural, geographic area (referred to in this part as a "community") . . .

(2) which provides services, assistance, and other activities of sufficient scope and size to give promise of progress toward elimination of poverty or a cause or causes of poverty through developing employment opportunities, improving human performance, motivation, and productivity, or bettering the conditions under which people live, learn, and work;

(3) which is developed, conducted, and administered with the maximum feasible participation of residents of the areas and members of the groups served;[37]

The mobilization of resources, the focus on the "community," and the mandated involvement of residents clearly follow from the adapted structural theory which saturated the Foundation and the Committee. The second section, which mentions services to improve human performance, motivation, and productivity appears to derive from another explanatory framework, but conceptual clarity was not absolute in the legislation.

John Wofford alludes to the increased intermingling of structural theory with "culture of poverty" concepts, but clarifies the position of the Community Action Program staff who remained with the new organization after its evolution from the Task Force.

Little thought, if any, was given by those of us who helped administer CAP to a distinction between poverty (a lack of money) and the "culture of poverty" (the life style that goes with poverty). If we had been forced to say which of these concepts was a more central target of CAP, we probably would have responded that the emphasis (and it was only a matter of emphasis) was on attempting to deal with the life style of the poor, but primarily through qualities in the environment – particularly institutions that affect that life style.[38]

Remember that the delegation of programs from the community action agency to existing institutions in the community seemed necessary to involve them in a self-renewal process leading to greater concern and action in behalf of the poor.

The *Community Action Program Guide* clarifies and expands the positions stated in the legislation. The latitude allowed to local communities is stressed, but the three concepts—a local base, coordination, and comprehensiveness—are reinforced throughout the document. Thus, from various sections of the *Guide*, statements such as those that follow instruct applicant communities in the policies of the Community Action Program:

A vital feature of every community action program is the involvement of the poor themselves – the residents of the areas and members of the groups to be served – in planning, policy-making, and operation of the program.[39]

Poverty is a condition of need, helplessness, and hopelessness. It is rooted in a network of social ills that include inadequate education, unemployment, poor health, and dilapidated housing. To alleviate them requires a varied and coordinated attack.[40]

The criteria for "Eligibility of Applicant" include the legal authority necessary to enter into contractual arrangements with the Federal Government,

The ability to mobilize and utilize the community's public or private resources in an attack on poverty.

A commitment to enlist the participation of residents of the areas and members of the groups to be served in the development, conduct and administration of the proposed program.

Adequate provision for participation in policy-making by the major agencies and institutions in the community, both public and private, which have a concern with poverty . . .[41]

These selected quotes, extracted from the more detailed requirements for funding (the specification for local share contributions, the differences in legal construction of public and private non-profit organizations, etc.), indicate the overriding concern of the social structural orientation, in the emphasis on the involvement of institutions and the repeated mention of participation by program consumers.

The frequent insistence upon the capacity to mobilize resources is the facet of the program which is used in the *Guide* to stress both comprehensiveness and coordination. Under a specific heading, "Mobilization of Resources," is the following suggestion:

Most agencies tend to concentrate on one basic service function, such as education, employment, health, housing, or family welfare. Where several agencies are working in the same functional area, they relate to each other in a "service system." The mobilization of resources for a community action program should bring these various service systems together in a concerted attack on poverty.[42]

No less than eight of these service systems are mentioned, each with its activities and goals distinct from other systems in the fragmented array of programs which the planners attacked. Their concern is reflected in a continuation of this section:

Each of these service systems deals with only part of the complex and interrelated causes of poverty. The separate service systems need to be linked in a total network in order to mount an effective attack on poverty. Each applicant agency must demonstrate its ability and intention to mobilize community resources against poverty through the establishment of linkages among and within service systems and through other means.[43]

This last statement can serve as the generic model developed by the Task Force planners. It includes the structural dysfunction concept in its focus on regulating service systems which are isolated from the poor and from one another. The various service systems were to be included in the policy-making and program operations of the community action agency as a means of reform-through-involvement. The program was to be comprehensive—another legislative requirement—through this inclusion of diverse service systems, and responsive to the needs of the poor because of the citizen participation requirement. This model, even with the "maximum feasible participation" clause, was approved by the Congress with little challenge. Other questions about its validity were left unanswered, perhaps even unrecognized.

One of the first signs of potential trouble for the local community action agencies appeared in the attempt to construct the President's Committee. Continual competition over funds, staff selection, and domain prerogatives prevented any meaningful coordination among federal level bureaucracies.

The inability to persuade quasi-autonomous units to surrender some of their independence to a more inclusive body—so vital to any coordinative structure—was an early reality to be either dealt with or rationalized away. It concerned David Hackett, the Executive Director of the President's Committee, who wrote a memorandum to the Attorney General stating,

While we have encouraged coordination in the local level, we are constantly hampered by the lack of a corresponding coordination of Federal programs. Fortunately, we have been able to develop informal arrangements with some of the Federal agencies to help meet the needs of our seventeen cities. But such arrangements are tenuous, are not carried on with an overall commitment to comprehensive programming, and are often endangered by bureaucratic haggling.[44]

Conflict over relative role, influence, and share of the new funds also provoked early disruption in the anticipated pattern of institutional coalescence at the local level. In one community after another, the member organizations of the new Ford Foundation or President Committee's (or both) agencies maintained their prior identifications, and refused conceptual or operational merger. Institutional self-interest, despite formal endorsement of the Committee's program, remained intact in several cities. In Cleveland, Chicago, Los Angeles, and Philadelphia the new projects were bogged down in old jurisdictional disputes which superceded the objectives and proposed innovations of the funding bodies. While the report did not come at the earliest stages of the new projects, accounts in several of the cities indicated that internecine struggles often preceded the actual implementation of programs planned with money from Ford or the President's Committee.[45]

The Community Action Program emerged as a potentially revolutionary stimulus to institutional change, but it was plagued by potential internal conflict which could have accounted for later compromises and/or failures. The new venture, radically different in its conceptual orientation, in its stipulations regarding local policy-makers, and in its primary strategy, became operational in August 1964. The next chapter will present data collected from community action programs in twenty cities across the nation. The purpose of the chapter is to compare what happened in the cities with what could have been projected from the planning of the Community Action Program. The program data is based upon all programs funded and administered in the twenty cities in the first two years of the poverty program (August 1964 to August 1966).

NOTES

[1] Economic Opportunity Act of 1964, Title IIA, Section 202.

[2] Levitan, Sar, *The Great Society's Poor Law: A New Approach to Poverty*, (Baltimore: Johns Hopkins Press, 1969), p. ix.

[3] Vatter, Harold G., *The U.S. Economy in the 1950's: An Economic History* (New York: W. W. Norton & Company, Inc., 1963), pp. 7–8.

[4] Marris, Peter, and Rein, Martin, *The Dilemmas of Social Reform* (New York: Atherton Press, 1967), p. 11.

[5] *Ibid*, pp. 20–21.

[6] Kravitz, Sanford L., "The Community Action Program — Past, Present, and Its Future," in *On Fighting Poverty*, James L. Sundquist, ed. (New York/London: Basic Books, Inc., 1969), p. 56.

[7] *Ibid*, pp. 58–59.

[8] Sviridoff, Mitchell, "Contradictions in Community Action," in *Psychiatry and Social Science Review*, Vol. 2 No. 10 (October 1968), p. 4.

[9] *Ibid*, pp. 19–20.

[10] *Ibid*, p. 21.

[11] *Ibid*, p. 22.

[12] Donovan, John C., *The Politics of Poverty* (New York: Western Publishing Company, 1967), p. 41.

[13] Marris and Rein, *The Dilemmas of Social Reform*, p. 2.

[14] Donovan, *The Politics of Poverty*, p. 35.

[15] *Ibid*, p. 41.

[16] Wofford, John G., "The Politics of Local Responsibility: Administration of the CAP — 1964–1966," in *On Fighting Poverty*, James L. Sundquist, ed. (New York/London: Basic Books, Inc., 1969), pp. 79–80.

[17] Marris and Rein, *The Dilemmas of Social Reform*, p. 215.

[18] Kravitz, "The Community Action Program — Past, Present, and Its Future," pp. 62–63.

[19] Conversation with Robert Lefferts, a member of the Task Force, (January 29, 1970).

[20] *Preliminary Report — Task Force on Urban Areas* — dated April 8, 1964, pp. 6–8.

[21] *Ibid*, pp. 25–26.

[22] *Ibid*, pp. 27–30.

[23] *Ibid*, pp. 19–22.

[24] Marris and Rein, *The Dilemmas of Social Reform*.

[25] Thernstrom, Stephen, *Poverty, Planning and Politics in the New Boston: The Origins of ABCD*, (New York/London: Basic Books, Inc., 1969).

[26] Mannheim, Karl, *Ideology and Utopia*, (New York City: Harcourt, Brace and Company, Inc., 1936), p. 40.

[27] Mannheim, *Ideology and Utopia*, p. 219.

[28] *Ibid*, p. 122.

[29] *Ibid*, pp. 144–145.

[30] *Ibid*, pp. 144–147.

[31] Interview with Robert Lefferts, January 23, 1970.

[32] Kravitz, "The Community Action Program. . . .", p. 60.

[33] *Preliminary Report — Task Force on Urban Areas*, p. 2.

[34] *Ibid*, p. 32.

[35] *Ibid*, p. 46.

[36] Economic Opportunity Act of 1964, Section 2.

[37] Economic Opportunity Act of 1964, Title II A, Section 202, numbers 1, 2, 3.

[38] Wofford, "The Politics of Local Responsibility . . .", p. 71.

[39] *Community Action Program Guide*, p. 7.

[40] *Ibid*, p. 7.

[41] *Ibid*, p. 14.

42 *Ibid,* p. 15.
43 *Ibid,* p. 16.
44 *Ibid,* pp. 135–136.
45 *Ibid,* pp. 156–157.

CHAPTER VII

Involvement—Commitment— and Reform? The Data from the Community Action Program

THE operational aspect of the Community Action Program will be the focus of this chapter. The data presented has accumulated from a study of citizen participation in twenty local community action agencies. The sampling process used to select these cities is described in full in Appendix A. Several major limitations imposed in sample selection, and several identifying characteristics of the cities, will be presented below. We shall also present information reviewing the federal regulations required of cities, the instructions set forth in the *Community Action Program Guide,* and the description of the participants in the development of the local Community Action Agencies. Later sections of the chapter will describe and analyze the "involvement" of the existing service systems, the allocative practices of the local Community Action Agency in relation to the service systems, and the degree of "commitment" and "reform" achieved through the program.

By the fall of 1966, when the study of "Citizen Participation in Community Action" was preparing to enter the field, nearly 1,000 American communities had created Community Action Agencies. The sample of twenty cities was selected from a total city population of sixty-eight. The criteria used to select the sixty-eight cities follow:

(1) The core urban community in which the Community Action Program was based must have had a population of at least 50,000.

(2) The Community Action Agency must have received a grant from the Office of Economic Opportunity for one program in addition to or other than Summer Head Start by June 30, 1965. (This was to insure that some planning processes at the local level had occurred, and that some comparability was available among the cities based on common time parameters.)

(3) The largest eligible cities such as New York, Chicago, or Los Angeles were excluded on the basis of their size. They were considered too large for thorough investigation.

(4) Eight other cities were excluded from the sample for a variety of reasons including logistics (Honolulu) and their inclusion in other OEO-sponsored research.

In the process of sample selection we tried to determine the possibility of ranking all of the sixty-eight cities on the variable of citizen participation in the local community action agency. Visits to the Washington and Regional OEO-CAP offices indicated that such a high-low division on this variable was not feasible. It became clear that the "maximum feasible participation of the poor" was a complex phenomenon, and that the classification system was inadequate since it artificially restricted the criteria for locating each city to only one dimension. Using available information, the research staff of the study was able to determine that a random selection from the population of 68 cities provided a range on several established variables. The staff based its decision to pursue random selection upon reviewing applications to OEO from the sixty-eight communities, noting the data on the participants in the policy-making processes of the local agencies and interviewing the Regional Office staff members most familiar with the cities.

Following the selection of the twenty cities, the characteristics of the sample cities were compared with the characteristics of all sixty-eight cities. The community profile factors developed by Jeffrey Hadden and Edgar Borgatta in *American*

Cities,[1] were used for comparison. The findings indicated that no significant differences appeared in the sample on any of the twelve variables used for comparison.

Table 1 lists the twenty cities and compares them on several variables including population, percent non-white, percent poor (according to the standard of $3,000 for a family of four), and median income. These dimensions have been selected as relevant to the problem of poverty and the potential attraction of federal funds. For purposes of comparison, the reader is provided with a ranking for each city on each variable. Note the range on each of these variables: 61,000–876,000 in population; 0.7–72.5% non-white; 10.9–51.0% poor; and, in median income, $2,935–6,949. The apparently substantial differences on these variables between the cities might seem important as determinants of our later outcome variables, the allocation of Community Action Program funds to agencies (via subcontracts), and the distribution of programs among the three social action strategies which were derived from the three Ideal Type explanations of the problem of poverty.

The remainder of this chapter is divided into five sections: a review of the OEO regulations regarding the establishment of a local community action agency, including the provisions for involvement of existing service systems; an analysis and description of the extent of involvement of the service systems using program delegation as the primary measurement; an analysis and description of the program data according to social action strategy; an attempt to identify variables which might serve as determinants of specified strategies; and conclusions.

INVOLVEMENT OF COMMUNITY SERVICE SYSTEMS

The planners of the Community Action Program developed an organizational strategy which called for involving the various local service systems in the community and *depended*

Table 1

The Twenty City Sample by Population, Percent Non-White, Percent Poor, and Median Income

City	Population (000's)	Rank†	Percent Non-White	Rank†	Percent Poor ($3000 base)	Rank†	Median Income	Rank†
Akron	290	7	13.1	13	13.1	14	$6466	16
Charlotte	202	10	28.0	6	21.0	9	5592	9
Chattanooga	130	13	33.2	4	31.5	2	4438	2
Cincinnati	503	4	21.8	7	19.6	10	5701	10
Cleveland	876	1	28.9	5	17.2	11	5935	12
Durham	78	17	36.3	3	27.9	3.5	4673	3
Flint	196	11	17.7	8	12.9	15	6340	15
Hartford	162	12	15.5	10	15.0	13	5990	13
Huntington	84	16	5.7	17	23.8	6	5426	8
Laredo	61	20	72.5‡	1	51.0	1	2935	1
Lorain	69	18	13.5‡‡	12	12.5	16	5908	11
Milwaukee	741	2	8.9	14	11.4	19	6664	19
Phoenix	439	5	14.9‡‡‡	11	16.8	12	6117	14
Providence	208	8	5.8	16	21.9	7	5069	7
San Antonio	588	3	48.8‡‡‡‡	2	27.9	3.5	4691	4
San Jose	204	9	17.3§	9	11.5	18	6949	20
St. Paul	313	6	3.0	18	11.8	17	6543	18
Scranton	111	14	0.7	20	21.1	8	5005	6
Waterbury	107	15	6.7	15	10.9	20	6535	17
Wilkes-Barre	64	19	1.3	19	25.0	5	4829	5

† Ranks ordered from highest to lowest
‡ 72.1% Mexican-American
‡‡ 7.0% Puerto Rican
‡‡‡ 9.1% Mexican-American
‡‡‡‡ 41.4% Mexican-American
§ 14.0% Mexican-American

upon these organizations' developing a commitment to help the poor. Anticipating local organizational commitment, the planners expected the local organizations to reform themselves voluntarily. The effort at reform focused on changing the problem definition and derived social action strategy. The agencies would have to shift from their traditional perspective, the Culture of Poverty ideal type, to a new perception of problems—the Social Structural ideal type.

The *Community Action Program Guide,* which instructed applicant cities how to organize their local community action agencies, contains the details of the planners' organizational strategy. Certainly a key component, emphasized both in publicity about the Community Action Program and in the administrative regulations, was the participation of poverty area residents:

The Economic Opportunity Act requires that a community action program be developed, conducted, and administered with the maximum feasible participation of the residents of the areas or neighborhoods in which the program will be carried out and of the members of the groups that it will serve.[2]

This guideline operationalizes the specification in the legislation—Title II A, Section 202(a) (3). Also found in the same document are the directions concerning the involvement of the network of existing agencies:

Most agencies tend to concentrate on one basic service function, such as education, employment, health, housing, or family welfare. Where several agencies are working in the same functional area, they relate to each other in a "service system." The mobilization of resources for a community action program should bring these various service systems together in a concerted attack on poverty.[3]

Table 2 describes the involvement of various sectors of the community or service systems in the development of the local community action agency. It accounts for those constituencies represented in the creation of the community action agency, in the development of the application for a program development grant, and in the preparation for the first program proposals. All of these actions preceded the appointment of the community action agency board and the formal creation of the local anti-poverty organization. The decisions made by this group, called the "initiators and developers," were carried out by the local community action agency.

In *none* of the twenty cities were any poor people, any representatives of the neighborhoods, or members of the groups to be served involved. Even such organizations as civil rights groups were also left out of the process at this stage of develop-

Table 2

Initiators and Developers of Community Action Agencies in Twenty Cities

City	Mayor's Office	Health and Welfare Council or United Fund	Board of Education	Public Agencies	Other
Akron	X	X	X		X
Charlotte		X	X		X
Chattanooga	X	X	X		
Cincinnati	X	X	X	X	X
Cleveland	X	X	X	X	
Durham		X			X
Flint	X		X	X	
Hartford	X	X	X		X
Huntington		X			X
Laredo	X		X	X	
Lorain	X			X	
Milwaukee	X	X	X	X	
Phœnix	X	X			X
Providence	X	X			X
San Antonio	X	X		X	X
San Jose		X	X	X	
Scranton	X		X	X	X
St. Paul	X	X			X
Waterbury	X	X	X	X	X
Wilkes-Barre		X			X
TOTAL	15	16	12	10	13

ment. While these groups appeared at a later date on the boards of directors of the local agencies, their participation frequently did not occur until the local agencies had started operating, had hired staff, and had secured both administrative and program budgets.

The existing network of service systems, however, was represented in generous proportions. The Mayor's office took part in developing the community action agency in fifteen of the twenty cities; the local Health and Welfare Council or United Fund was involved in sixteen of the twenty cities; the Board of Education was involved in twelve cities; various public agencies such as the Welfare Department were involved in ten of the cities; and other established local organizations such as the City Council, local universities, labor councils, and churches were involved in thirteen cities.

In eight of the cities (Akron, Cincinnati, Cleveland, Hartford, Milwaukee, San Antonio, Scranton, and Waterbury) at least four of the major "service systems" or agency domains were represented; in eight of the cities (Charlotte, Chattanooga, Flint, Laredo, Phoenix, Providence, San Jose and St. Paul) three of the domains were involved; and in four of the cities (Durham, Huntington, Lorain, and Wilkes-Barre) two of the organizational domains were involved.

When the distribution of programs is examined and related to the institutional systems which participated in the initiation and development of the initial programs, the benefits of "involvement" are clear. Table 3 describes the distribution of all community action programs funded in the twenty cities during 1964, 1965, and 1966 according to the administering (program operating) agency. Given the local option of having the community action agency administer its own programs or delegate programs to sponsoring agencies by subcontract, either the new organization or the existing agencies were eligible to receive funds. In each of the cases listed here, where an organization other than the community action agency is the implementing or administering organization, it was given a contract(s) by the community action agency which approved its proposal and submitted it to OEO for funding.

In the Table, grants for establishing the community action

Table 3

Distribution of Community Action Programs by Administering Agency (Excludes Administrative Grants to Maintain CAA)

City	Total Number of Community Action Programs & Percent Administered by CAA		Board of Education	Voluntary Social Agencies	Community Action Agency	Public Agencies	Ethnic and Religious Agencies	Other
	Number	Percent						
Akron	20	15.00	10	1	3	2	1	3
Charlotte	16	37.50	5	4	6	1		
Chattanooga	12	16.66	6	2	2	2		
Cincinnati	44	2.27	19	19	1	4	1	
Cleveland	33	18.18	7	19	6		2	
Durham	12	75.00	3		9			
Flint	9	0.00	6	2				1
Hartford	32	3.13	14	11	1	5		1
Huntington	8	50.00	2	2	4			
Laredo	10	10.00	1	3	1	1	2	2
Lorain	5	40.00	3		2			
Milwaukee	19	0.00	10	8			1	
Phoenix	12	33.33	5	1	4	1	1	
Providence	23	47.83	4	7	11			1
San Antonio	28	7.14	6	4	2	1	14	1
San Jose	13	53.85	2	2	7	1	1	
Scranton	8	12.50	5	2	1			
St. Paul	15	0.00	5	7			3	
Waterbury	19	57.89	6	2	11			
Wilkes-Barre	12	16.66	3	5	2		2	
TOTAL	350		122	100	73	19	28	8
Percent of Total	100.00		34.86	28.57	20.86	5.43	8.00	2.29

agency, in which funds were used for administrative purposes required to set up and maintain the organization, were excluded as they could not possibly have been delegated to other agencies.

Once again, using program distribution as an output measure, we can see the impact of the initiators and developers on overall program allocation. Involvement of the existing organizational network occurred to such an extent that the local community action agency administered less than twenty-one percent of programs funded under its auspices in the twenty cities studied. The range of the percentage of programs administered directly by the local community action agency (as opposed to those delegated to other organizations) runs from 0–75, with only eight cities having community action agencies administering 20 percent or more of the community action programs funded through the local anti-poverty agency. The Board of Education was represented in all twenty cities; voluntary social agencies received contracts in eighteen; public agencies received contracts in nine; and ethnic and religious agencies received delegated contracts in ten. In three cities, the community action agency administered none of its own programs, while in four others the local community action agency ran only one program. Across the twenty cities, the mean number of programs was 17.50, while the mean number of community action agency administered programs was 3.65 —less than 21 percent.

Another, perhaps more significant, way of measuring the "involvement" of local organizations is to analyze the financial allocations of the local community action agencies—which organizations received funds to administer the community action programs? Table 4 depicts this budget breakdown according to program auspices. It portrays which organizations received the money from OEO through the conduit of the local community action agency. Table 5 presents the same information, but the figures represent the percentage of the

total program budget of each city (minus administrative
grants to the community action agency) allocated to each
category of "involved" agency.

Table 4

Distribution of Community Action Program Funds (in 000's)
by Administering Agency
(Excludes Administrative Grants to Maintain CAA)

City	Total Program Budget	Board of Education	Voluntary Social Agencies	Community Action Agencies	Public Agencies	Ethnic & Religious Agencies	Other
Akron	2032	1230	68	529	85		120
Charlotte	2308	1184	476	589	59		
Chattanooga	1642	997	37	322	286		
Cincinnati	4768	2675	1845	38	210		
Cleveland	6440	2405	2639	934		462	
Durham	1408	349		1059			
Flint	346	282	53		11		
Hartford	2284	1376	363	293	237		15
Huntington	513	154	156	203			
Laredo	1300	166	525	7	315	112	175
Lorain	162	98		64			
Milwaukee	3484	2366	1081			37	
Phoenix	2166	910	81	1023	102	50	
Providence	4928	3200	551	1124			53
San Antonio	3190	561	283	13		2245	88
San Jose	3951	580	933	2109	287	42	
Scranton	1127	1000	114	13			
St. Paul	1944	949	933			62	
Waterbury	1368	581	138	649			
Wilkes-Barre	485	180	247	24		34	
TOTAL	45,846	21,243	10,523	8,993	1,592	3,044	451
PERCENT OF TOTAL	100.00	46.33	22.95	19.62	3.47	6.64	.98

Table 5

Percentages of Program Budgets Allocated to Local
Agencies by the CAA

City	Total Program Budget (000's)	Board of Education	Voluntary Social Agencies	Community Action Agency	Public Agencies	Ethnic & Religious Agencies	Other
Akron	2032	60.53	3.35	26.03	4.18		5.90
Charlotte	2308	51.30	20.62	25.52	2.56		
Chattanooga	1642	60.72	2.25	19.61	17.42		
Cincinnati	4768	56.10	38.70	.80	4.40		
Cleveland	6440	37.34	40.98	14.50		7.17	
Durham	1408	24.79		75.21			
Flint	346	81.50	15.32		3.18		
Hartford	2284	60.25	15.89	12.83	10.38		.66
Huntington	513	30.02	30.41	39.57			
Laredo	1300	12.77	40.38	.54	24.23	7.71	13.40
Lorain	162	60.49		39.51			
Milwaukee	3484	67.91	31.03			.98	
Phoenix	2166	42.01	3.74	47.23	4.71	2.31	
Providence	4928	64.94	11.18	22.81			1.02
San Antonio	3190	18.53	8.87	.41		70.38	2.76
San Jose	3951	14.68	23.61	53.38	7.26	1.06	
Scranton	1127	88.73	10.12	1.15			
St. Paul	1944	48.82	47.99			3.19	
Waterbury	1368	42.47	10.09	47.44			
Wilkes-Barre	485	37.11	50.93	4.95		7.01	
TOTAL	45,846						

The capacity of the Board of Education to become "involved" in the local community action agency appears even more clearly when we review the budget data. Even though the Board of Education was involved as an initiator and developer in only twelve of the cities, it received contracts from all twenty local community action agencies, and in total commanded 122 of 350 programs (approximately 35 percent) and over 46 percent of the total Community Action Program budget as expended in the twenty cities. Recall that this significant inroad into the Community Action Program was made even though the school systems were a primary target for reform in the minds of the Community Action Program planners. The data leave no doubt about the engagement of this institution. Later information regarding the purposes for which the money was spent may challenge the notion that the Board of Education was in any way reformed.

Despite the attacks by the nascent Community Action Program on the social work profession, it, too, managed to survive, if not thrive, on the monies channeled into the localities through the anti-poverty agencies. Voluntary social agencies, the bulwark of the social work profession (such as settlement houses, family service-type agencies and others), garnered 100 programs across the twenty cities (approximately 29 percent) and approximately 23 percent of all program funds. In fact, the voluntary social agencies attracted more funds than the local community action agencies were able to generate for their own program operations. This is indicated in the comparison of the community action agencies with voluntary social agencies and the Board of Education:

Organization	CAP Funds	Percent of Total
Board of Education	$21,243,000	46.33
Voluntary Social Agencies	10,523,000	22.95
Community Action Agencies	8,993,000	19.62

Here, as with the schools, involvement was assured in at least eighteen of the twenty communities where the traditional social agency service system was delegated Community Action Program funds.

Before moving onto an analysis of all 350 programs, we shall describe how the Board of Education, the voluntary social agencies, and the community action agencies spent their funds. The programs have been divided into nine categories: pre-school, other educational services, social services, health services, legal services, National Emphasis programs—services (Medicare, Alert, Project Enable), income producing programs, institutional change oriented programs, and other programs.

Of the 122 programs contracted with the various educational systems, 99 were either pre-school (70) or other educational services programs (29). Local Boards of Education also ran nineteen social service programs in five cities, two health programs, and two other programs. In a more detailed breakdown of the anti-poverty activities of the educational systems, the Boards of Education administered,

70 of the 86 pre-school programs
29 of the 38 other educational services programs
19 of the 145 social services programs
2 of the 13 health programs
2 of the 8 other programs.
_____
122 Total

Voluntary social agencies administered 100 programs, spread over seven of the program categories:

6 of the 86 pre-school programs
1 of the 38 other educational services programs
71 of the 145 social services programs
11 of the 14 legal services programs
8 of the 25 National Emphasis-service programs
1 of the 10 income producing programs
2 of the 11 institutional change oriented programs.
_____
100 Total

Settlement houses, health and welfare councils, day care centers, recreation agencies, casework agencies, and legal aid agencies were all represented in the distribution of programs across the twenty cities. The social work profession did not remain aloof from the local action in the local war on poverty despite Sargent Shriver's biting criticism of the profession in a speech delivered to the 1965 National Conference on Social Welfare.[4] As with the schools, the initial stage in the planners' strategy of involvement, commitment, and reform was achieved in relation to the social services system.

Given the major participation of these two service systems in the anti-poverty program, the local community action agencies rarely were able to administer their own program operations. When the local community action agencies did administer community action programs, they were in the following categories:

> 1 of the 86 pre-school programs
> 3 of the 38 other educational services programs
> 30 of the 145 social services programs
> 3 of the 13 health services programs
> 2 of the 14 legal services programs
> 14 of the 25 national emphasis services programs
> 7 of the 10 income producing programs
> 9 of the 11 institutional change oriented programs
> 4 of the 8 other programs.
> ———
> 73 Total

This broad distribution represents a different emphasis in programs from those administered by the other two major recipients of Community Action Program funds—the school system and the social agencies. While very few total programs either of an income producing or an institutional change oriented nature were created, 70 percent of the former and almost 82 percent of the latter were operated by the local community action agency. We shall trace below this significant departure in programming as we move on to discuss programs in terms of the distribution among the three social action strategies.

Each of three ideal type explanations of the problem of poverty in America had a logically related social action strategy as one of its components. For a brief recapitulation, the ideal types and the derived strategies are presented here:

Ideal Type	*Social Action Strategy*
Culture of Poverty	Individual and Cultural Change
The Dysfunctional Social System	Institutional Change
The Dysfunctional Economic System	Directed Change in Economic Policy

We assume that all of the programs developed under the aegis of the Community Action Program can be categorized into these three basic strategies for eliminating the poverty problem in our society.

Kenneth Clark and Jeannette Hopkins, in a recent book about the War on Poverty,[5] describe its services as compatible with the Individual and Cultural Change strategy which is based upon a culture of poverty explanatory model:

Services: Help through services from the community of affluence to the community of need. The tradition of services is the traditional foundation of social welfare, both public and private, with the public agencies tending toward alleviation of gross need (abject poverty-relief checks; psychosis-hospitalization; delinquency-recreation), and the private agencies oriented toward individual casework (impending divorce-family counselling), though both engage in both activities and, in many ways, parallel each other's function. This is essentially a paternalistic approach to need that assumes the persistence and inevitability of need . . .[6]

This type of program intends to bring about changes in the individual or in small groups of individuals. It focuses attention on their behavioral deficiencies, value differences, or both, and deflects concern away from the social structure or present societal conditions. This is accomplished through using the concept of deviance, which contains an implicit concept of normality (the socially prescribed behavior), or through the concept of "subcultural values" which implies deviance from the approved or legitimate social order.

The object of the social service and individual change strategy is the individual or his reference group (a small number of individuals). Thus, all pre-school programs which focus on bringing the lower class child up to the level of the middle class child; all remedial and other educational service programs which seek to raise the level of the individual; all counselling, psychiatric or social work programs which seek to help the individual either change his behavior or adapt to his environment (the existing social structure); and all programs which segment part of the individual's life as a focus for lifting him out of poverty (health services, legal services, family life education, family planning) form the operational structure of the Individual and Cultural Change or Social Service strategy.

The problems of the poor the Dysfunctional Social System ideal type defines as logically derived adaptations to the frustrations imposed by lower class allegiance to the broader cultural structure when goal achievement in terms of that cultural order was barred by social structural obstacles. Foremost among those obstacles is the lack of power held by the lower class. Power is considered necessary to confront the social institutions which perpetuated the problems faced by the poor. In this view, unresponsive city halls, school systems, social agencies, employment services—the society's institutions—must be confronted by organized constituencies of the poor, who together could generate the political power to press their own demands upon the social system and by so doing, change the system. Clark and Hopkins refer to programs of institu-

tional change as "social action programs," which they define
as based on the following assumptions:

that poverty is caused by a condition of powerlessness; that poverty
will continue to exist until the poor gain the power necessary to
reverse their present condition; that collective action must be initiated, based on organizations of the poor who identify their problems, design strategies, and maintain themselves when confronted
with conflict; and that such organizations must state their goals in
terms of observable changes in communities or in the conditions of
the poor.[7]

Community or neighborhood organization programs, consumer
action, community development, resident participation, and
resident employment programs are all considered working
expressions of the Dysfunctional Social System explanatory
model.

Clark and Hopkins, having spent a year in the field and having detailed reports on community action programs, differen-
tiate community organization from community or social action
programs by the focus of concern. Community organization
programs, which they relate to the social work tradition, still
concern the individual or the small group organized to redress
some current condition (e.g., neighborhood clean-up) which
they have created. Social action programs, on the other hand,
focus on the structural component in the creation and perpetuation of problems afflicting the poor. This study recognizes
and accepts this distinction, but did not have the resources to
delineate one form of organizational effort from the other. As
a result, we have grouped both under the program strategy of
Institutional Change.

The Dysfunctional Economic System or Economic Mismanagement Ideal Type directs its social action strategy at national
level economic policy changes; no major change is required
in the social structure or institutional control of the society.
Since these policy alterations have clear objectives—to raise

the level of income of the poor—we can describe locally developed programs related to this approach. Called income producing programs, they include such projects as finding jobs, developing jobs, and Nelson Amendment (employment) programs.

Having examined the operational derivatives of each of the three ideal types, we remind the reader of the affinity of the national Community Action Program planners for the Dysfunctional Social System explanation of the problem, its institutional change strategy, and the planners' ideal that with involvement of the existing service systems would come "commitment" to their model. This in turn would lead to "reform" from within the organizations which made up the service systems to program orientations consistent with the social structural paradigm.

The data presented below will depict the numbers of programs allocated to each of the three social action strategies, the budget allocation among the three alternative strategies, and the social action strategy followed by each of the major constituencies represented in the distribution of programs (the Board of Education, the voluntary social agencies, and the local community action agency). To be consistent with the planners' expectations, a large proportion of funds should have been allocated to social action programs or programs which have institutional change as their goal. Table 6 shows the distribution of Community Action Programs by strategy.

The data stand in stark contrast to the programs which one might have projected from the Community Action Program planners' definition of the poverty problem. In eleven cities the social services strategy completely dominated programs, while only six cities even attempted any form of institutional change strategy. If we use percentages to measure the same phenomena, eleven cities had 100 percent social service programming, and in only one city out of the twenty was there

Table 6

Distribution of Community Action Programs by Strategy
(*Percentages and Total Programs Omit Administrative Grants*)

City	Total Number of Programs	Service Strategy Focus		Income Strategy Focus		Institutional Change Strategy Focus	
Akron	20	20	(100.0)				
Charlotte	16	14	(87.5)	1	(6.3)	1	(6.3)
Chattanooga	12	12	(100.0)				
Cincinnati	44	44	(100.0)				
Cleveland	33	32	(94.1)			1	(2.9)
Durham	12	10	(83.3)	1	(8.3)	1	(8.3)
Flint	9	9	(100.0)				
Hartford	32	32	(100.0)				
Huntington	8	6	(75.0)			2	(25.0)
Laredo	10	9	(90.0)	1	(10.0)		
Lorain	5	5	(100.0)				
Milwaukee	19	19	(100.0)				
Phoenix	12	10	(83.3)	1	(8.3)	1	(8.3)
Providence	23	22	(95.7)	1	(4.3)		
San Antonio	28	28	(100.0)				
San Jose	13	10	(76.9)	3	(23.1)		
Scranton	8	8	(100.0)				
St. Paul	15	15	(100.0)				
Waterbury	19	12	(63.2)	2	(10.5)	5	(26.3)
Wilkes-Barre	12	12	(100.0)				
TOTAL	350	329		10		11	
PERCENT OF TOTAL	100.0	93.73		2.85		3.13	

less than 70 percent social service or individual and cultural change programming. The social service strategy underlay approximately 94 percent (329 out of 350) of all the programs, while the income producing strategy underlay slightly less than 3 percent (or 10 of the 350 programs) and the institutional change strategy—the logically derived or expected outcome—underlay only *slightly more than 3 percent* (11 out of 350) of all Community Action Programs conducted in the twenty cities in 1964–1966.

The study conducted by Clark and Hopkins reinforces the findings presented above. They have nine program categories, all of which can be subsumed under the three major strategies. Data from the Clark-Hopkins study appears below. Their classifications of the programs of fifty-one cities are presented in Table 7. Table 8 shows the same data reordered into the three major orientations of this study.

The comparisons between the distribution of Community Action Programs in our twenty city sample and the fifty-one city sample of the Clark–Hopkins study are as follows:

	Total Programs	Percent Services	Income	Institutional Change
20 City Sample	350	93.73	2.85	3.13
51 City Sample	405	84.69	9.88	5.43

The reason for the closeness in total number of programs, despite the gulf between the sample sizes, arises in part because the present study covers a three year period from 1964–1966, while the Clark–Hopkins data is based upon a one year sampling of programs in 1965. The two studies show no major differences: the overwhelming proportion of programs in both samples focused on change within individuals and/or within small groups of individuals and did not direct attention to the society within which those people live.

Table 7

*Classification of Fifty-one Community Action Programs
in Terms of Services* [8]

(1)   EDUCATIONAL SERVICES
    41   Head Start
    32   Compensatory, enrichment programs
    10   "Cultural deprivation" programs
    12   Adult education programs
     8   Teacher training programs
     7   Educational counseling and guidance
     6   Work study programs
   116 – Total

(2)   SOCIAL SERVICES
    23   Group work and recreation programs
    16   Multi-service centers, comprehensive school centers, or
         umbrella programs
    16   Homemaker services, including consumer education
    13   Day care
    10   Casework services
     9   Family planning programs for unwed mothers
     8   Arts and culture programs
     6   Welfare services
     2   Mental health programs
   103 – Total

(3)   SPECIFIC DELINQUENCY PREVENTION AND
     CONTROL SERVICES
     4 – Total

(4)   HEALTH SERVICES (No narcotics programs mentioned)
    23 – Total

(5)   HOUSING SERVICES
    10 – Total

(6)   LEGAL AID SERVICES
    8 – Total

(7)   JOB TRAINING AND PLACEMENT SERVICES
    11   Job counseling

9   Job training
8   Economic self-help, programs for small business
6   Work study programs (also included under (1))
6   Skills development and vocational training
5   Adult employment, upgrading, experience
3   OJT programs
3   General upgrading of skills
1   Youth work experience

52 – Total

(8) COMMUNITY ORGANIZATION PROGRAMS
15   Organization for program involvement
12   Organization in neighborhood centers
7   Traditional social welfare-settlement house style organizations

34 – Total

(9) COMMUNITY ACTION
23   Use of indigenous staff
12   Use of indigenous community groups
10   Indigenous leadership training
5   Organization for action
5   Indigenous community representation on boards

55 – Total

SUMMARY

Services		*Community Organization*		*Community Action*	
1. Educational	116	All forms of community organization	34	Leadership training	10
2. Social services	103			Indigenous participation	40
3. Job training and self-help	52			Organization for action	5
4. Health services	23				
5. Housing	10				
6. Legal aid	8				
7. Delinquency	5				
TOTAL – 317		TOTAL – 34		TOTAL – 55	

The program data clearly contradict the intended structural change orientation of the national Community Action Program planners; if the service programs are coupled with the income producing programs in the twenty city sample, 97 percent of all locally developed and approved Community Action Programs had little relationship to the concept "community action." This compares with approximately 95 percent in the Clark–Hopkins study. The relationship which did exist was

Table 8

Reclassification of the Clark-Hopkins Program Categories

I. Directed Individual/Cultural Change = 343 Total Programs (Social Service Approach)

   (1) *Educational Services*

      41 Head Start
      32 Compensatory enrichment programs
      10 "Cultural Deprivation" programs
      12 Adult education programs
       8 Teacher training programs
       7 Educational counseling and guidance
       6 Work study programs
       9 Job training
       6 Skills development and vocational training
       3 General upgrading of skills
      ——
      134 – Total

   (2) *Social Services*

      23 Group work and recreation programs
      16 Multi-service centers, comprehensive school centers or umbrella programs
      16 Homemaker services, including consumer education
      13 Day care
      10 Casework services
       9 Family planning programs for unwed mothers
       8 Arts and culture programs
       6 Welfare services
       2 Mental health programs
       4 Delinquency prevention and control services
      23 Health services
      10 Housing services

      8 Legal aid services
     11 Job counseling
      6 Work study programs
     15 Organization for program involvement
     12 Organization in neighborhood centers
      7 Traditional social welfare-settlement house style
          organizations
     10 Indigenous leadership training
    ___
    209 – Total
    ___
    343 – Total Individual/Cultural Change Programs
  II. Income Producing Programs = 40 Total Programs
      8 Economic self-help
      5 Adult employment, upgrading experience
      3 OJT programs
      1 Youth work experience
     23 Use of indigenous staff
    ___
     40 – Total
 III. Institutional Change or Social Action Programs = 22 Total
      Programs
     12 Use of indigenous community groups
      5 Organization for action
      5 Indigenous community representation on boards
    ___
     22 – Total

administrative—local agencies, and to a lesser degree, the community action agency itself used the funds of the Community Action Program to continue the social service strategies which they had previously tried to implement.

Ironically, the same strategies had served the national Community Action Program planners as a rationale for a change needed in the societal definition of the poverty problem. The transformation required in problem definition was apparent in the planners' rhetoric, in the Task Force papers, and in the mandated participation of the local residents and members of the groups served. Neither the groups intended in the rhetoric about participation, nor the action strategies planned to assist them, appeared to have had much influence in the allocation of anti-poverty funds.

Table 9 shows the distribution of Community Action Program funds among the three alternative social action strategies. As expected from the data on program distribution, the service

Table 9

Distribution of CAP Funds by Program Strategy
(Percentages are for Programs Only and Omit Administrative Costs)

City	Total Budget (000's)	Service Strategy	Income Strategy	Institutional Change Strategy	Administrative Costs
Akron	2224	2032 (100.0)			192
Charlotte	2472	1932 (83.7)	293 (12.7)	83 (3.6)	164
Chattanooga	1755	1642 (100.0)			113
Cincinnati	5022	4768 (100.0)			254
Cleveland	6880	6323 (98.1)		117 (1.8)	440
Durham	1677	1301 (92.4)	52 (3.6)	55 (3.9)	269
Flint	458	346 (100.0)			112
Hartford	2601	2284 (100.0)			317
Huntington	669	369 (71.9)		144 (28.0)	156
Laredo	1453	985 (75.7)	315 (24.2)		153
Lorain	228	162 (100.0)			66
Milwaukee	3791	3484 (100.0)			307
Phoenix	2511	1550 (71.5)	229 (10.5)	387 (17.8)	345
Providence	5532	4673 (94.8)	255 (5.1)		604
San Antonio	3341	3190 (100.0)			151
San Jose	4511	2981 (75.4)	970 (24.5)		560
Scranton	1242	1127 (100.0)			115
St. Paul	2089	1944 (100.0)			145
Waterbury	1703	818 (5917)	377 (27.5)	173 (12.6)	335
Wilkes-Barre	650	485 (100.0)			165
Totals	50809	42396	2493	959	4963
(Administrative Costs)	— 4963				
	45846				
Percentages	100.0	92.47	5.44	2.09	

strategy overwhelmingly dominates the field. In view of this
social service domination, Moynihan's criticism of the Community Action Program as a failure predicated upon the in-
accurate problem definition of the national level planners is
as indefensible as his charge that the local programs were
dominated by racial or professional militants.[9] The professionals from both the education and social welfare fields proved
to be politically accomplished as well as durable, for they were
able to capture over 92 percent of the monies to be used in
reforming their "establishments." As demonstrated in the
tables above, the existing local organizational network was
very "involved."

The acts expected to follow—commitment and reform—
were forsaken in the transformation of problem definition. As
the planners' national strategy and conceptual analysis of the
problem gave way to traditional agency application at the local
level, defects in the social order became redefined as deviance
in the lower class. Consistent with the change in definition of
the problem was a change in the social action strategy designed
to counteract it. The institutions at the local level, as integral
parts of the social structure, transformed the institutional
change strategy to guarantee their own survival by redirecting
the focus onto the client group and away from the institutional
order. The evidence for this statement, as extracted from the
data: 96 percent of all programs and 98 percent of all funds
went to support programs which derived from a definition of
the problem differing from that maintained by the national
Community Action Program planners.

The expenditures by various administering agencies in relation to the three strategies are in order:

Percent of Program Strategy

Organization	Percent of Programs	Percent of Funds	Service	Income	Institutional
Board of Education	34.86	46.33	100		
Voluntary Agencies	28.57	22.95	97	1	2
Community Action Agency	20.86	19.62	78	10	12
Public Agencies	5.43	3.47	89	11	
Ethnic & Religious	8.00	6.64	100		
Other	2.29	.98	100		

The next section will attempt to associate a number of independent variables with the degree of service strategy. In the data, we noticed one especially strong association—that between the degree of community action agency self-administered programs and the likelihood of operating a total program with an approach other than 100 percent service strategy. Dividing the cities into two groups on each of the two variables, those with 100 percent services (eleven cities) and those with less than 100 percent services (nine cities), and those with 20 percent or less community action agency self-administered programs versus those with more than 20 percent self-administered programs, yields and following correlations:

		Percent Service Strategy	
Percent of	More than	*100%*	*Less than 100%*
CAA-	20% CAA-run	1	7
administered	Less than		
Programs	20% CAA-run	10	2

Since the category, "less than 100 percent service strategy," need only mean that a local community action agency operated one income producing *or* one institutional change oriented program, the association can be interpreted to indicate that when the local interorganizational network was extricated from program operation, some chance for strategies other than social services was available. Given the expectation of five cases in each cell above, this is quite likely. If it is compared with the 100 percent service strategy of the Board of Education (no income producing or institutional change programs), the 97 percent service strategy (one income producing and two institutional change programs out of 100) of the private social agencies, and the breakdowns of the other sponsoring agencies, the threat of the community action agency's disrupting the problem definition and strategies of the traditional agency systems is clear.

But once dominated by subcontractual arrangements and a coordinative organizational structure which included the traditional service systems, the local anti-poverty agency became a clearing house for funding programs designed to enhance or expand the domain of cultural and individual change oriented services presided over by the Board of Education, the private social agencies, the public agencies, and the ethnocentric agencies. It was very difficult to move beyond the level of "involvement" to commitment and reform within the local service systems included in the organizational strategy of the planners. The continuity in problem definition and related social action strategy had been maintained by the traditional agency systems, which were able to use the local community action agency as a conduit for newly available funds. Reform from within of this local interorganizational network of organizations had conclusively failed.

VARIATIONS ON A THEME—
RANDOM DISTRIBUTION

In an attempt to predict or understand potential determinants of the two major dependent variables—distribution of Com-

munity Action Programs among the three possible social action
strategies and percent of community action agency-administered programs—we shall associate several variables with the
data on program distribution. First, we shall relate city size
to social action strategy. In Table 10 the twenty cities are
arrayed according to size, and compared with both the social
action strategy analysis and with the percent of community
action agency-administered programming. One can clearly
see that the programs classified into the three social action

Table 10

*City Size as a Determinant of Program Strategy Outcome
and Percent CAA-Administered Programs*

| City | Size (000's) | Percent of Social Action Strategies (by budget) | | | Percent CAA Admin- istered Programs |
		Service	Income	Institu- tional Change	
Cleveland	876	98.1		1.8	18.18
Milwaukee	741	100.0			0.00
San Antonio	588	100.0			7.14
Cincinnati	503	100.00			2.27
Phoenix	439	71.5	10.5	17.8	33.33
St. Paul	313	100.00			0.00
Akron	290	100.00			15.00
Providence	208	94.8	5.1		47.83
San Jose	204	75.4	24.5		53.85
Charlotte	202	83.7	12.7	3.6	37.50
Flint	196	100.00			0.00
Hartford	162	100.00			3.13
Chattanooga	130	100.00			16.66
Scranton	111	100.00			12.50
Waterbury	107	59.7	27.5	12.6	57.89
Huntington	84	71.9		28.0	50.00
Durham	78	92.4	3.6	3.9	75.00
Lorain	69	100.00			40.00
Wilkes-Barre	64	100.00			16.66
Laredo	61	75.7	24.2		10.00

strategies and the percent of programs administered directly by the community action agency were randomly distributed over the twenty cities. The major association revealed in this table is between the percentage of community action agency-administered programs (using 20 percent and above as "high") and the development of strategies other than services. This association, which we outlined above, holds up despite substantial variation in city size.

The next variable examined in search of a significant determinant of social action strategy is ethnic composition. This dimension deserves particular attention in view of the accusation that OEO and the Community Action Program, in particular, were specifically designed for the militant black population. If this piece of popular wisdom were true, we should expect higher per capita expenditures in those cities where there are the highest percentages of black population, and where the institutional change strategy is most often used.

Table 11 destroys these myths, and rules out the percentage of non-whites as a significant determinant of either strategy outcome or program administration. It also contradicts the notion that the Community Action Program was specifically or generally designed for any one ethnic group. Laredo, which has a population 72.5 percent non-white but only 0.4 percent black, nevertheless ranks second in per capita Community Action Program funds attracted; Providence, which ranks first in per capita CAP funds, has a population only 5.8 black. In contrast, Chattanooga, which ranks second in proportion of black population, has a 100 percent service strategy and ranks seventh in per capita funds; while Cleveland, which ranks fifth in percentage of black population, operated a 98.1 percent service strategy and ranked thirteenth in per capita funds. The dependent variables are randomly distributed on the percentage of city population, non-white variable, just as they were on city size.

Table 11

Percentage of City Population Non-White as a Determinant of
Program Strategy Outcome and Percent
CAA-Administered Programs

City	Non-White (%)	Percent of Strategies			CAA-Run Programs (%)	Per Capita CAP Expenditures
		Service	Income	Institutional Change		
Laredo	72.5	75.7	24.2		10.00	$23.82
San Antonio	48.8	100.0			7.14	10.67
Durham	36.3	92.4	3.6	3.9	75.00	21.50
Chattanooga	33.2	100.0			16.66	13.50
Cleveland	28.9	98.1		1.8	18.18	7.85
Charlotte	28.0	83.7	12.7	3.6	37.50	12.24
Cincinnati	21.8	100.0			2.27	9.98
Flint	17.7	100.0			0.00	2.34
San Jose	17.3	75.4	24.5		53.85	7.67
Hartford	15.5	100.0			3.13	16.06
Phoenix	14.9	71.5	10.5	17.8	33.33	5.72
Lorain	13.5	100.0			40.00	3.30
Akron	13.1	100.0			15.00	7.64
Milwaukee	8.9	100.0			0.00	5.12
Waterbury	6.7	59.7	27.5	12.6	57.89	15.92
Providence	5.8	94.8	5.1		47.83	26.60
Huntington	5.7	71.9		28.0	50.00	8.32
St. Paul	3.0	100.0			0.00	18.82
Wilkes-Barre	1.3	100.0			16.66	10.16
Scranton	0.7	100.0			12.50	6.09

The last demographic characteristic to be associated with
the program strategy variable and the percent community
action agency-administered program variable is the percent of
poor in the city (using an income standard of $3,000 for a
family of four). Table 12 shows the relationship of this variable to program strategy outcome, percent of community
action agency-administered programs, and per capita Commu-

nity Action Program funds. As with the other two demographic variables, the percent of poor shows no significant relationship to any of the dependent variables. The distribution of program strategies and percent of community action agency-administration of programs in relation to this variable is random.

Table 12

Percent Poor in the City as a Determinant of Program Strategy Outcome, Percent CAA-Administered Programs, and Per Capita CAP Funds

City	Percent Poor	Social Action Strategies			% CAA-Administered Programs	Per Capita CAP Funds
		Service	Income	Institutional Change		
Laredo	51.0	75.7	24.2		10.00	23.82
Chattanooga	31.5	100.0			16.66	13.50
Durham	27.9	92.4	3.6	3.9	75.00	21.50
San Antonio	27.9	100.0			7.14	10.67
Wilkes-Barre	25.0	100.0			16.66	10.16
Huntington	23.8	71.9		28.0	50.00	8.32
Providence	21.9	94.8	5.1		47.83	26.60
Scranton	21.1	100.0			12.50	6.09
Charlotte	21.0	83.7	12.7	3.6	37.50	12.24
Cincinnati	19.6	100.0			2.27	9.98
Cleveland	17.2	98.1		1.8	18.18	7.85
Phoenix	16.8	71.5	10.5	17.8	33.33	5.72
Hartford	15.0	100.0			3.13	16.06
Akron	13.1	100.0			15.00	7.64
Flint	12.9	100.0			0.00	2.34
Lorain	12.5	100.0			40.00	3.30
St. Paul	11.8	100.0			0.00	18.82
San Jose	11.5	75.4	24.5		53.85	7.67
Milwaukee	11.4	100.0			0.00	5.12
Waterbury	10.9	59.7	27.5	12.6	57.89	15.92

Local Organizational Involvement as a Determinant of Program Strategy, Percent CAA-Administered Program, and Per Capita Attraction of Funds

City	Percent Program Strategies			Percent CAA-Administered Program	Per Capita CAP Funds
	Service	Income	Institutional Change		
4 or More Local Service Systems Involved					
Akron	100.0			15.00	7.64
Cincinnati	100.0			2.27	9.98
Cleveland	98.1		1.8	18.18	7.85
Hartford	100.0			3.13	16.06
Milwaukee	100.0			0.00	5.12
San Antonio	100.0			7.14	7.14
Scranton	100.0			12.50	6.09
Waterbury	59.7	27.5	12.6	57.89	15.92
Mean Percent	94.73	3.44	1.8	15.01	
3 Local Service Systems Involved					
Charlotte	83.7	12.7	3.6	37.50	12.24
Chattanooga	100.0			16.66	13.50
Flint	100.0			0.00	2.34
Laredo	75.7	24.2		10.00	23.82
Phoenix	71.5	10.5	17.8	33.33	5.72
Providence	94.8	5.1		47.83	26.60
San Jose	75.4	24.5		53.85	7.67
St. Paul	100.0			0.00	18.82
Mean Percent	87.64	9.63	2.66	24.90	
2 Local Service Systems Involved					
Durham	92.4	3.6	3.9	75.00	21.50
Huntington	71.9		28.0	50.00	8.32
Lorain	100.0			40.00	3.30
Wilkes-Barre	100.0			16.66	10.16
Mean Percent	91.08	.90	7.98	45.42	

The next determinant is the extent of involvement of the local organizational networks or service systems. We shall explore this by grouping the twenty cities into three subgroups: those having four or more of the major service systems involved in the initiation and development of the local community action agency; those having three sectors involved; and those having two sectors involved. We shall then associate the cities within these three categories with the resultant variables as we did with the preceding variables. Table 13 presents this information.

No important differences appear between the three subgroups in terms of service strategy (the mean percentages being 94.73 for the category with four service systems; 87.64 for the category with three service systems; and 91.08 for the category with two service systems). The extent of the social service strategy domination across all cities indicated that these findings would occur. Two important differences in mean scores do stand out, however. The cities with only two of the local service systems involved as developers and initiators of community action agencies showed a much higher tendency to administer local programs than did the other two categories. The mean percent of community action agency-administered programs for this group was 45.42, almost twice the score (24.90) for the subgroup with three local service systems involved, and more than three times the mean percent (15.01) for the category containing four local service systems.

Remember the strong association between the percentage of community action agency-administered programs and the likelihood that programs will be developed out of conceptual schemes other than the Culture of Poverty. The data support the assertion that the less the involvement of the existing service systems at the local community level, the greater the likelihood that non-service strategy programs will be developed. This hypothesis appears to act even more strongly with regard to the institutional change strategy: 50 percent of the subgroup with two service systems carried out institutional change oriented programs, compared to 25 percent of each of the other two categories. The respective mean percentages for each group in the institutional change strategy column are 7.98 for the two service system categories, and 2.66 and 1.8 for the other two categories respectively.[10]

CONCLUSIONS

The conclusiveness of the data makes repetition of dubious value. It will suffice here to reiterate the four major hypotheses and to examine them with the perspective provided by the data. The first hypothesis is,

The higher the level of coordination of existing agencies from the horizontal system, the lower the level of program administration by the local community action agency.

This assertion appears to be an accurate account of the situation in the twenty cities of the sample. Criteria for this hypothesis consisted of representation in the group of initiators and developers, and the degree of program delegation from the local community action agency to organizations which are included in the existing service systems of the community. The mean percent of community action agency-administered programs for those local community action agencies initiated and developed by four or more community service systems was 15.01, compared to 24.90 for community action agencies with three service systems involved in the initiation and development stage. The figure was 45.42 percent for community action agencies with only two service systems represented. Thus, the greater the number of service systems involved as initiators and developers, the greater the percentage of programs contracted out to the organizations which make up the service systems, and the smaller the percentage of community action programs operated by the local anti-poverty agency itself.

The second hypothesis indirectly involves relationships between the local community action agency and the Regional or Washington office of the Community Action Program. It reads,

The greater the involvement of organizations from the horizontal system (in the community action agency creation and initial program development), the more effective the community action agency in attracting OEO-CAP funds.

This hypothesis was not proven. The data used to attest to this fact indicate that the subgroup of the community action agencies with four service systems involved in initial organizational activities attracted a mean per capita funding of $9.48. The category with three service systems involved attracted a mean per capita funding of $13.86 and the last category, with two service systems involved, had a mean per capita figure of $10.82. Implicit in this second hypothesis is the assumption that the vertical system—the Regional and Federal OEO-CAP offices—condoned both the level of local autonomy in program administration allowed the community action agencies by their local service systems and the type of programming which this eventually produced.

This proved not to be the case, as often the Regional or Federal Community Action Program offices intervened in the communities, on behalf of low income people, to negotiate acceptable levels of citizen participation on the community action agency boards or advisory committees with the initiating and proposal developing group ("initiators and developers"). In other cases, where delegate agencies from one or another of the existing service systems proposed a "community action" type program (institutional change strategy) but operated the program with the individual-small group change approach, the Regional Community Action Program office again intervened and terminated the subcontract.[11]

Participation in policy-making was entirely determined within the local community in the initial phase of development. When controversies emerged over board membership (at a later date, frequently in 1965–66, after the initial community action agency structure and program had been determined), OEO often intervened as advocates for the poor.

The third hypothesis, relating to social action strategy and definition of the problem, is,

The greater the involvement of organizations from the horizontal system, the greater the likelihood of an Individual-Group Change Strategy and the less the likelihood of the Institutional Change or Income-Producing strategies.

In all twenty cities the involvement of the existing service systems which make up the local horizontal system was substantial and exerted a major influence in predisposing the social action strategy of the community action agency toward the Individual-Group Change orientation. Eleven of the cities had 100 percent of their programs derive from the Culture of Poverty explanatory model with its social services approach to problem solving. Of the remaining nine cities, three had between 90–99 percent service programs, five had between 70–89 percent, and only one had below 70 percent.

With this Social Service domination of available options as a background, a tendency still emerged within the twenty cities which supports the contention in the hypothesis: a mean percent of programs which fell within the institutional change strategy was calculated for each of the three categories delineated by number of service systems involved in the "initiators and developers" group. The category with the fewest service systems involved had a mean percent of 7.98 compared to 2.66 and 1.80 for the other two subgroups respectively. Furthermore, given the relationship between community action agency autonomy and increased likelihood of income producing or institutional change programs, and the differentiation between the subgroups on the variable of community action agency autonomy, the hypothesis appears to be substantiated.

The proof of this hypothesis appears in the overwhelming evidence that the conceptual scheme and social action strategy designed by the national Community Action Program planners were overturned or transformed by the local service systems. In place of the planners' model, institutions promoted a contradictory strategy (and, therefore, a contradictory explanation of the poverty problem) at the local level. These organizations captured over 80 percent of all program funds and determined the strategy for approximately 97 percent of all programs.

The next chapter will analyze the transformation of the Community Action Program from the problem definition and social action strategy developed by the federal level planners of the Community Action Program to that of the local anti-poverty warriors.

NOTES

[1] Hadden, Jeffrey K., and Borgatta, Edgar F., *American Cities: Their Social Characteristics*, (Chicago: Rand McNally and Company, 1965).

[2] *Community Action Program Guide*, p. 16.

[3] *Ibid*, p. 15.

[4] Shriver, Sargent, "Poverty in the United States — What Next?", *The Social Welfare Forum — 1965* (National Conference on Social Welfare; New York and London: Columbia University Press, 1965).

[5] Clark, Kenneth B. and Hopkins, Jeannette, *A Relevant War Against Poverty: A Study of Community Action Programs and Observable Social Change* (New York and Evanston: Harper and Row Publishers, 1969).

[6] *Ibid*, p. 27.

[7] *Ibid*, p. 36.

[8] *Ibid*, pp. 64–65.

[9] Moynihan, *Maximum Feasible Misunderstanding*, p. 136.

[10] Statistical treatment was intentionally left out of this chapter as we felt that the data can be clearly understood in tabular form.

[11] An excellent example of this situation is related to the contract given by the Cleveland Anti-Poverty Agency to the Greater Cleveland Neighborhood Centers Association. OEO-CAP insisted the program be discontinued or absorbed *by the community action agency* itself. A similar set of circumstances appeared in San Antonio with programs supposedly designed to assist migrants. The contract with the delegate agency was terminated and the program turned over to the community action agency.

CHAPTER VIII

Power, Perception, and Program—an Analysis of the Transformation of the Community Action Program

INTRODUCTION

PLANNING a program of social action was a complex process. At the national level it involved developing a definition of the problem to be remedied and creating a model organization to implement the strategies which flowed from the problem definition. It also involved countless hours of meetings to deliberate the course of action to be taken with the overall Poverty Task Force, Congressional committees, and other constituencies. Planning demanded enormous energy in administrative affairs from those of the Task Force on Urban Areas who went on to work for the new Community Action Program of the War on Poverty.

Although the author does not know the details of the planning process at the local level, the results indicate that much local effort was involved in determining the response: aligning the relevant actors; generating staff assistance in proposal development; and negotiating a consensus among the relevant organizations in the community regarding who would initiate and develop the local agency, who would be empowered to set policy, and who would receive contracts using the newly available Federal funds. Even though both Federal and local officials were engaged in planning programs to eliminate poverty, the outcomes of the processes turned out to be substan-

tially different. This chapter will attempt to explain the reasons
for that difference.

It is ironic that organizations, which are said to abhor uncertainty, exist in an uncertain context, the interorganizational
field in the local community and in the broader society. To
understand the transformation of the Community Action Program as it moved from the planning phase at the national level
to the operational phase at the local level, we must devote
attention to the context in which Community Action Programs
were to be run. Remember that the CAP planners did not
focus on this issue as a critical one in their planning. Rather,
they assumed that the organizations which have come to pro-
liferate in American community life and to perform the necessary functions of communities voluntarily would become involved in the anti-poverty effort. They further believed that
these organizations would modify their practices and policies
to conform with the Community Action Program in its problem
definition and social action strategy. These basic assumptions
appear unwarranted in view of available evidence, and the
failure of the social action strategy calling for institutional
change through voluntary, internal reformulation of problems
can be traced to this oversight.

The uncertainty forced upon any local organization (or national organization) in American communities comes from the
absence of any overall, authoritative structure. Warren describes this complex situation:

communities are made up of numerous formal structures (city government, industries, labor unions, private agencies, for example)
and interaction patterns rather than being constituted as a single
organizational unit with comprehensive power and decision-making
authority.[1]

Warren developed an interest in the operations of large community organizations after analyzing American communities and their increasing reliance on formal organizations to perform the functions necessary for communal living. Through time, these organizations were sanctioned to operate in specified spheres of activity on behalf of the community. Warren concluded that the interorganizational field at the local level consisted of an increasing number of city-wide or metropolitan level organizations, each of which was legitimated or given approval to carry out planning and/or programming in a particular sphere of community activities. In most cases, these organizations received a significant proportion of their funds from the Federal government, which also had varying influence over their program development activities. Interaction between these organizations seems inevitable because of a scarcity of either input or output resources. Thompson makes note of this fact of organization life, describing how organizations are necessarily involved with their environments in acquiring the input resources required by their technologies and in dispensing their products or services among an unpredictable output constituency.[2]

Norton Long has developed a similar concept of organizational interaction at the community level. In his view, the local community approximates an "ecology of games," interaction is unplanned, yet largely functional. Long sees the community as a natural system which "is the product of a history rather than the imposed effect of any central nervous system of the community."[3]

In line with this view of the community, Long asserts that there is no dominant power source capable of directed social planning and change. Long emphasizes this point:

The bases of power are not only split within the city, the splits are multiplied by the multiplicity of jurisdictions and the lack of any centripetal metropolitan institutions. The answer to the question

"Who Governs?" . . . is quite literally nobody. The system after a fashion runs. Nobody runs it.[4]

In this unstructured and fluctuating environment, organizations must attempt to conduct their operations and negotiate settlements. The crucial issue to be resolved with other organizations is the domain, or functional relationship of any organization to its environment. Thompson defines a domain as claims which an organization stakes out for itself in terms of (1) problem area covered, (2) population served, and (3) services offered.[5]

The process of establishing a domain is a political one, requiring the establishment of dependencies (for input resources such as finances, staff, and legitimation) and the development of an explanatory mechanism to organize the personnel around the negotiated domain. The establishment of a viable domain engages the organization with the local ecological order or, in Thompson's words, the local "domain consensus," "a set of expectations both for members of an organization and for others with whom they interact, about what the organization will and will not do."[6]

The entrance onto the stage of a new organization, with the dynamics of the territorial stage at work, appears as a crisis for existing organizations and for the domain consensus negotiated over time. Long notes that along with an awareness of organizational boundaries within the system is a pattern of interaction and rules about the players of the game, the roles held by each party, and the mode of communication.

When a new organization brings with it an unclear set of domain expectations, regulations insisting on new participants in the local game, and undetermined methods of organizational interaction, the domain consensus within the community is unsettled. This was clearly the case with the Community Action Program. The CAP carried its own rhetoric of institutional change, comprehensive programming, and participation of the poor in the local agency structure, which it had attacked as being a partial cause of the problems the CAP sought to eliminate. The comprehensive thrust of the anti-poverty effort involved itself immediately in the domain concerns of every service system.

The rhetoric about institutional change created uncertainty beyond geographic or output constituency concerns as organizations responded to threats to their technologies (or services offered). And the new rules involving participation aroused further concern over the relationship between the organization and its control over output elements. Thus, from the beginning, the Community Action Program threatened all three components of an organization's domain—the services offered, the legitimation to operate in a protected problem area, and the population served. Long has developed a prescription for organizational action in response to such threats to their survival: "The need or cramp in the system presents itself to the players of the games as an opportunity for them to exploit or a menace to be overcome." [7]

The planners of the Community Action Program provided the local organizations with both an opportunity and a menace. The opportunity was clearly to increase their independence from local financial constraints by capturing the newly available Federal funds. The menace was the constraints and impositions on organizational autonomy which had previously been negotiated with other organizations—the domain consensus.

Thus, the creation of a community action agency posed two great threats: on one level, a challenge to the individual organization's domain; on another level, an impending change in the local territorial system or domain consensus. Because of these conditions, and the circumstances of unplanned interaction between the various segments of community activity (service systems or, in Long's terminology, games), the situation could have been very uncertain. The potential for change in such circumstances was great, because organizational rationality could not function in such an open or unstable environment. Rationality can only exist in circumstances where organizations can control relevant variables and respond in fixed patterns to previously calculable contingencies. Neither of these controls existed in the problem definition and institutional change strategy of the Community Action Program planners. The possibility of achieving the goal of institutional change was enhanced by creating flux or turbulence in the interorganizational field and forcing the organizations into confronting uncertainty in unreliable ways.

But such change in the interorganizational context was not to occur. The organizational model designed by the CAP planners, stipulating the involvement of existing service systems, created an organizational framework which reduced uncertainty by channeling the decisions required to create the new agencies through the filtering device of coordinated planning. By including the interorganizational field within the organizational structure of the new community action agency, the Community Action Program planners provided the opportunity to recreate the local domain consensus or reinforce it with Federal funds. The collaboration of the existing system was documented in the data on involvement of service systems found in Chapter VII.

We have also noted the degree to which the interorganizational field was involved in creating the new agency and in developing its original program proposals. The purpose of the local interorganizational collaboration, as the data on program allocation and program strategy makes clear, was to preserve the domain consensus in the face of the newcomer's threat. Recall that approximately 80 percent of the programs developed through the local community action agency and approximately 80 percent of all Community Action Program funds were delegated to existing organizations. Further, almost 98 percent of these funds were spent on programs which came from an explanatory model contradicting the original planners' framework.

We can understand the capacity of the interorganizational field to dominate the decision-making of the new agencies by investigating the role of the "initiators and developers" of any new organization. Christopher Sower, *et al.*[8] found that the two crucial determinants of any action on social problems were: the constituencies represented by the initiators and the relationship of the proposed action to existing definitions of community welfare.

According to Sower and his associates, furthermore,

It is through a convergence of interest arising out of values, beliefs, and relationships of the larger community that a group is formed which is concerned with the initiation of a specific action. Until such a formation takes place, action exists only in the minds of individuals. The establishment of such an initiating set leads to the development of a common frame of reference from which concrete action flows.[9]

We can take the common frame of reference to which Sower and his associates refer as the domain consensus worked out by the initiators and developers. The boundaries established for the new action are confined to the problem definition determined by this group and to the allocation of resources among those authorized to operate programs stemming from the agreed upon definition. This process of definition and legitimation removes uncertainty from the interorganizational field, decreasing the turbulance created by the threat of institutional change.

We have seen that the various service systems in the community either were convened by the Mayor or constituted themselves as the local "initiating set." The influence of these groups on the final outcome of the local community action agency was described in the program data presented in Chapter VII. The greater the involvement of the interorganizational field, the lower the level of autonomy of the community action agency. Related to community action agency autonomy was social action strategy (and through implication, definition of the problem)—the greater the autonomy of the community action agency, or the lower the involvement of the interorganizational field in the initiation set, the greater the likelihood of a program based on a strategy other than individual or cultural change.

The experience of the Community Action Program has demonstrated that the power to influence a program's outcome is largely determined by the actions of the initiation set in creating and developing the local action arena or in establishing the domain for the new organization within the interorganizational field. This phenomenon was obvious in the data from the twenty cities in this study. This locus of power raises critical question about capacity of existing institutions to legislate and plan local social change or to predict the outcome of a local program based on a Federal design. Investing power and authority in the existing service systems to involve themselves in their own reform seemed eventually to contradict the institutional change strategy. Reform did not come forth, as uncertainty was reduced by the regulations governing the structure of the community action agency. The actors powerful enough to join the group of initiators and developers of the new organizations turned out to be the primary beneficiaries of its resources.

At the time of the establishment of the community action agency, the relevant actors in the environment were the power holders previously legitimated to perform negotiated services in the community. The dependencies created by these organizations resulted in a community action agency which generally reinforced the domain consensus which they had previously worked out over time. The evolution of the organization was predetermined by the originating commitments made by the initiators and developers in their own interests. The involvement of these groups was required, and the results were predictable. In overlooking the organizational reality, the planners created the demise of their own grand scheme.

The social base of the community action agency, the initiators and the developers of the organization, was further represented in the decision-making structure of the organization through membership on the board of directors. This inclusion within the input constituency (see Chapter I for a discussion of this term) of the community action agency prevented the scope of conflict from spreading to new actors and confined it to the competitive yet cooperative interaction of established organizations.[10] The collaboration of these competing organizations indicated that the competition would emerge within an overall framework of cooperation, or mutual adjustment between the organizations involved. The effect of the domination of the input constituency of the community action agency by existing service systems was to create a quasi-closed system in which the previous forms of competition over resources were maintained.

Relative power was maintained in proportion to the security of each organization's domain. Thus, the principal beneficiary, the organization with the highest degree of domain autonomy, was the Board of Education; the second beneficiary, the voluntary social service agencies. Interference in this process by the Office of Economic Opportunity could be marginal at best. Constraints—on the composition of the local agencies' boards of directors—were compromised by the organizational need to allocate funds authorized by the Congress, and by political pressure from the local governments when the political equilibrium (the domain consensus) was threatened in fact as well as in theory.

The role of the Federal and Regional offices in initial and later problem definition and selection of programs is an area of vital interest for further research. For present purposes, we need only note that while local autonomy is allegedly disappearing from American community life, the Community Action Program experience serves as testimony to the continued hegemony of local institutions in the face of threats from the vertical system to reform them through rationally planned social change.

While it is beyond the scope of this study to engage in an extensive theoretical discussion of the potential for planned social change, a brief departure from the analysis of the Community Action Program is merited by the questions raised in the CAP experience. Despite documented efforts which demonstrate that centrally planned, comprehensive social change is more a facet of the planners' training and orientation than empirically documented examination would merit,[11] the planners' insistence on its validity is maintained. Thus, coordination of existing service systems has developed out of the Community Council era, to be included in the Ford Foundation, President's Committee, Community Action, and now the Model Cities programs. The evidence from this study indicates that such collaboration between existing agencies serves to thwart reform and innovation rather than sponsor them.

Planners seem unable to reconcile rationality with political reality. As Thompson points out, planning is based upon certain rational assumptions about the context of American communities. Planning proceeds as if these communities were closed systems wherein contingencies as well as identifiable variables were fully known and controllable. Yet James Wilson clearly indicates that the power necessary to maintain such control, quite aside from the requisite knowledge regarding all contingencies, is unavailable in our social system.[12]

Why then are these myths perpetuated and allowed to remain the basis for American social policies? Why did such astute thinkers as the Community Action Program planners succumb to these myths at the cost of their planned strategy for bringing about institutional change? While the author does not presume to answer these complex questions adequately, he will offer a partial suggestion.

The ontological foundations of social planners seem rooted in a pluralistic assumption about the distribution of power in American society. Communities are said to be governed by interest groups which have legitimated domains of primary concern, but which can still be brought together in a rational manner to act in the "public interest" which overrides their specific concerns. Because of the total distribution of power among these easily identifiable sources, planning becomes a rational process of bringing these powerful actors together around a point of mutual concern and persuading them of the import and rationality of the planners' strategy. The theory assumes that they will act accordingly on the changes or infringements on institutional prerogitives that are implied. The pluralistic sources of power are not only considered rational, but even altruistic. The planning process becomes, therefore, primarily a technological matter, bringing needed resources to bear on identified social needs. This notion comes from Robert Agger and his associates:

Pluralists take the position, specifically or implicitly, that . . . major decisional options are not shaped by a ruling elite so much as they are by "technical" factors which, assuming there is a desire for "functional rationality," would lead rational men to similar choice situations or decisional outcomes, regardless of socio-economic class or official position.[13]

The vital ontological issue posed by these men is related to the assumption that men are rational. For the pluralists further believe that *a* best course of action exists and that it can be reached by technically or scientifically derived agreement.

The foundation of such beliefs is rooted in an ideology pervasive in this society which serves to bring about a "consensus" within the population where none in fact exists.[14] The façade

of consensus is required to maintain the present form of economic and political structure which benefits the few at the
expense of the vast majority. Ideology, in Mannheim's sense,
prevents this fact from becoming widely known by providing
a definition of reality which legitimates the existing power
arrangements. Pluralism is one such definition that has substantial credibility because it appears to offer the opportunity
to acquire influence and to wield power to those who really
have neither. It promises to represent those who are not actually represented in the mythological competition said to char-
acterize American society.

The influence of this ideology on rationality becomes clear
when we examine its influence on planners. For them, the
dictates of pluralism are unquestioned. The assumption of an
altruistic rationality among the institutions of the social structure also exists a priori. Thus, even for the Community Action
Program planners, who addressed the condition of powerlessness, the concept they generated was based upon a pluralistic
rather than a class-based model of conflict. They wanted to
create for the poor a competitive rather than a conflict oriented
base of social power. Their strategy called for the organizations of the poor to take their place at the negotiating table of
rational, altruistic organizations in working out the reforms the
existing institutions would have to undergo in responding to
what was clearly the "public interest." The power of an ideology, blatant in these circumstances, is captured by Irving
Horowitz:

By expanding our definition of the function of ideology to make
room not only for justification (Marx) and rationalization (Weber),
but also for the role of ideology in organizing and institutionalizing
social drives, one can more readily understand the binding force
of an ideological complex upon a social structure.[15]

As an operational arm of the ideological complex, planning
becomes the technology for extending social control through-

out all sectors of society. When planning deals with social problems it functions to control those causing the "problems" —as defined by the institutions of the society. Planning thus serves to allocate the defined deviants to the legitimated management or control institutions. In this study, the educational systems and social service systems were the social control agencies which received the benefits of the Community Action Programs.

Using this unusual format to return to the transformation of the Community Action Program, we see the problem definition constructed by the planners as a counter-ideological posture. It charged the existing institutional order with failure to respond to the needs of the poor, and asserted that this failure was the result of powerlessness—the poor lacked the power to pressure the organizations. The Community Action Program planners' definition of the problem also departed from the traditional therapeutic concept or personal deviation orientation of the institutional structure.

The convergence of the institutions' desire for continuity in the existing order and their interest in the individual or subcultural deviation approach to social problems is understandable. With the onus of responsibility for change on the individual or his peers, the management or control institution—as part of the social structure—is guaranteed a superior power position in relation to its clientele. This conceptual position functions to maintain the existing power arrangements and allocation of resources.

The Community Action Program planners' view modified slightly the problem definition, and in doing so it can be characterized as a "liberal-humanitarian" version of utopian thought. Their thinking was utopian in that it suggested a counter-ideological definition of reality based on contemporary social conditions, but it also neglected aspects of political reality in its organizational strategy and is classified accordingly. The Community Action Program planners' adherence in their organizational strategy to the ideological explanation of social change can be explained by C. Van Nieuwenhuijze's statement: "Faith makes the rational system watertight." [16]

The Community Action Program in its transformation shows the convergence of power, perception and program. The power position held by the organization employing the planner serves as a determinant of his perception of the problem. As this perception becomes operationalized through the planning process, programs coming from it are created. The covert function of these programs is to reinforce the power position of the organization.

We can impute this power-maintaining circle of power, perception, and program to the Community Action Program experience to understand the action of the local organizations in their almost universal adoption of the Culture of Poverty ideal type, in the construction of programs based upon an Individual and Cultural Change strategy, and in the perpetuation of poverty in America. We must relegate the belief that reform of the existing institutional order can be rationally planned, or that significant change can be effected from within the organizational structure of power, to the level of ideology and to the purpose of social control.

NOTES

[1] Warren, Roland L., "The Interorganizational Field as a Focus of Investigation," *Administrative Science Quarterly,* Vol. 12 No. 3 (December 1967), p. 401.

[2] Thompson, *Organizations in Action,* p. 20.

[3] Long, Norton E., "The Local Community as an Ecology of Games," in Norton E. Long, ed., *The Polity,* (Chicago: Rand McNally and Company, 1962), p. 139.

[4] Long, Norton E., "Community Decision-Making," in *Community Leadership and Decision-Making,* University of Iowa Extension Bulletin, No. 842, p. 6.

[5] Thompson, *Organizations in Action,* p. 26.

[6] *Ibid,* p. 28.

[7] Long, "The Local Community as an Ecology of Games," p. 144.

[8] Sower, Christopher; Holland, John; Tiedke, Kenneth; and Freeman,

Walter, *Community Involvement,* (Glencoe: The Free Press, 1957).

⁹ *Ibid,* p. 68.

¹⁰ Schottschneider, E. E., *The Semi-Sovereign People,* (New York: Holt, Rinehart, and Winston, 1960).

¹¹ See, for example, Banfield, Edward C., *Political Influence,* (Glencoe: The Free Press, 1961); Meyerson, Martin and Banfield, Edward C., *Politics, Planning and the Public Interest,* (Glencoe: The Free Press, 1955); Selznick, Philip, *TVA and the Grass Roots,* (Berkeley: University of California Press, 1953); Marris, Peter and Rein, Martin, *The Dilemmas of Social Reform,* (New York: Atherton Press, 1967); Eckstein, Harry, *The English Health Service* (Cambridge: Harvard University Press, 1964); Thernstrom, Stephen, *Poverty, Planning, and Politics in the New Boston: The Origins of ABCD,* (New York: Basic Books, Inc., 1969).

¹² Wilson, James Q., "An Overview of Planned Change," in Robert Morris, ed., *Centrally Planned Change,* (New York: National Association of Social Workers, 1964).

¹³ Agger, Robert E.; Goldrich, Daniel; and Swanson, Bert E., *The Rulers and the Ruled,* (New York: John Wiley and Sons, 1964), p. 76.

¹⁴ Horowitz, Irving L., "A Formalization of the Sociology of Knowledge," in Irving L. Horowitz, ed., *Professing Sociology: Studies in the Life Cycle of a Social Science,* (Chicago: Aldine Publishing Company, 1968), p. 68.

¹⁵ *Ibid,* p. 73.

¹⁶ Van Nieuwenhuijze, C. A. O., *Society as Process,* (The Hague: Mouton and Company, 1962), p. 114.

CHAPTER IX

Epilogue

It is customary to conclude research on social problems with statements about the implications of the study and suggested courses of action which might follow. Often, such recommendations are made in program terms. But programs are not the answer to the problems posed and the issues raised in this work. As mentioned earlier, the rush to create new programmatic responses often prevents the planner from fully understanding the failure of his previous efforts at planned social change. Rather than pursue what I consider to be a fruitless enterprise, I will devote the concluding few pages of this study to an examination of alternative roles which might be taken by planners committed to social justice through the eradication of poverty.

Efforts to consider alternative roles for planners have frequently been labeled "advocacy planning." But advocacy planning all too often shares with more traditional planning an ideologically rooted ontology. In "Advocacy and Pluralism in Planning,"[1] for example, Paul Davidoff articulates the advocate planner's role; his description of the new function of planners could easily include the actions taken by the Community Action Program planners. The advocacy planning posture also assumes the pluralistic distribution of power, the potential for rationally planned social change, and the capacity of an institutional system to reform itself either through the inculcation of new interpretations of the public interest or through new competitive political power within the pluralist framework.

The analysis of the Community Action Program in transition

leads this author to reject the advocacy role on the same basis that he rejects the traditional planning tasks. The ideological foundation of the value system of the planners, clearly supported by the increasing technological inputs into their professional training, can lead only toward system-maintaining plans. Rationality, in this ideological framework, becomes a goal or an end in itself rather than a process of logically developing operational strategies consistent with socially constructed definitions of the problem. The focus required is neither on programs nor rationality, but rather on the analysis of ideology and its impact on social policy.

This assessment of the problem suggests action to be taken: the education or resocialization of planners. This is a necessary first step toward moving beyond the constraints of system-maintaining ideological premises. The distribution of power and wealth in America must be reevaluated. Alternatives to the pluralist's definition of reality, such as those posed by Mills [2] or Gamson,[3] establish a counter-ideological ontology as a foundation for authentic social policy.[4] Authenticity is determined by the rational construction of social policy recommendations and programs founded on counter-ideological definitions of reality. The authenticity of these policies develops from the convergence of the policy intention and the interests of the people to be served. When the existence of the present form of political and economic structure of the society serves as the premise for the delineation of social policy, as in America today, authentic social policy cannot be created.

The implementation of authentically constructed and therefore counter-ideological social policies will not necessarily involve the existing institutional structure. By-passing the present organizational structure obviously requires the development of substantial power among those who are supposed to receive the benefits of existing policies, but do not. In order for power to be generated among those individuals and groups who are not now represented in decision-making, and for this power to be used in their own interests, counter-ideologies must replace the existing ideology widely found in all strata of American society. Until the ideological analysis and interpretation of class-based self interest are communicated to those now asserting their potential political interests, the emergent power groups will ratify and legitimize the existing structural distribution of power. Emergent power groups are currently serving this ratifying function in a number of cities which received Model Cities grants. Model neighborhood residents who organized themselves into "counter-vailing" boards routinely process proposals which guarantee the domain security of the existing institutional order.

Planners can have an effective authentic impact upon the future course of social policy development only when they are able to depart from their present ideological foundations. Following this necessary shift in ideology, they must make a commitment to the intended recipients of social policy. With this group as his constituency, the planner's function becomes one of ideological analysis, social policy formulation, and political organization. He delineates the causal assumptions behind existing policies and programs, relates these to the interests of his constituency, constructs authentic alternatives and develops consistent organizational models to achieve group goals. A planner operating on "authentic" ideology could discuss, for example, the causal explanation of the problem implicit or explicit in the Head Start Program, acknowledge the convenience and amenity in having pre-school education available, point out its irrelevance to the eradication of poverty, begin the discussion of alternative or additional programs (in the case that the constituent group wants to continue) and outline forms of organizational structures less amenable to co-optation by the existing service systems. The availability of alternative definitions of the problem based on counter-ideological foundations allows people contending for power a choice in their concrete actions and overall direction which is not presently available to them. It is the assumption of this author that, possessing clearly articulated alternatives, people will take authentic actions.

If the planning function is revised in this way, the education of the planner also requires adjustment. Obviously, the focus of his education shifts away from technology and toward increased study of the social sciences and their philosophical foundations. Developing an authentic educational experience in planning, however, may be difficult, for the same groups who control the social structure of America control the universities. Actions parallel to those suggested for groups not now represented in the community distribution of power are thus also critical in the universities. Student representation in the selection of faculty, control of curriculum, and educational policy are the goals of the counter-ideological student or faculty member.[5] This constituency must also recognize a counter-ideological definition of reality, for, without such an alternative theory it, like the emergent power groups, would be co-opted.

NOTES

[1] Davidoff, Paul, "Advocacy and Pluralism in Planning," *Journal of the American Institute of Planners*, Vol. 31 No. 4. (November 1965).

[2] Mills, C. Wright, *The Power Elite*, (New York: Oxford University Press, 1959).

[3] Gamson, William A., "Stable Unrepresentation in American Society," *American Behavioral Scientist*, Vol. 12 No. 2 (November–December 1968).

[4] The concept of authenticity is based upon Amitai Etzioni, *The Active Society: A Theory of Societal and Political Processes*, (New York: The Free Press, 1968). The author is indebted to Robert Lefferts for the creative use of the concept in a specific social policy context.

[5] Rose, Stephen M., "School and Social Reality," paper presented at the Annual Meeting of the Society for the Study of Social Problems, San Francisco (August 31, 1969).

Appendix A

Determining who qualified for the status, "poor," proved an arduous task. If, as Coser suggests, personal declaration of poverty is sociologically irrelevant, it also is bureaucratically inconceivable. Mollie Orshansky, from the Office of Research and Statistics in the Social Security Administration, is perhaps the most widely cited source of data about the poor; she notes, "Despite the nation's technological and social advance, or perhaps because of it, there is no generally accepted standard of adequacy for essentials of living except food."[1] Anthony Downs, an economist, conducted a study of the urban poor and presented the following finding:

Poverty in the United States is officially measured by a fixed standard of real income based upon the cost of a minimal human diet. . . . Any household is officially defined as "poor" by the Social Security Administration if its annual money income is less than three times the cost (in current prices) of a minimal diet for the persons in that household. In 1967, the "poverty level" for a four-person household was $3,335.[2]

In 1966 the poverty threshold figure was $3,130. In 1962 the Council of Economic Advisers set the figure at $3,000 and considered any four-person family with income under that figure to be poor. Thus, several different figures are used by different reporters to establish parameters for that segment of the American population living in poverty. The different criterion figures and the different time periods for various studies account for variations in the estimated number of poor families and individuals; e.g., Herman Miller puts the number at 7 million families,[3] and the Council of Economic Advisers at 9.3 million,[4] even though they use similar sources.

The tables below provide a sociological picture of the poor. They present various facts which run counter to the widespread but uninformed conventional wisdom regarding the poor:

— *Families headed by a woman are subject to a risk of poverty three times that of families headed by a man, but they represent only a fourth of all persons in families classed as poor.*[7]

— *Many of our aged have inadequate incomes, but almost four-fifths of the poor families have someone under age sixty-five at the head.*[8]

— *Nonwhite families suffer a poverty risk three times as great as white families do, but seven out of ten poor families are white.*[9]

— *About 47 percent of all poor in metropolitan areas (over one-half of all poor persons in the United States) are in households that cannot expect to become economically self-sustaining at any time in the future. These households include:*

Elderly	*18.9%*
Disabled males under 65	*6.4%*
Females under 65 with children	*21.3%*
	46.6% [10]

— *Nearly one-third of all poor persons in metropolitan areas (31.4%) are in households headed by employed men under sixty-five whose poverty results from low earnings rather than unemployment, disability, or old age.*[11]

— *About half of the poor families are still headed by neither*

Table 2

Selected Characteristics of all Families and of Poor Families, 1962 [5]

Selected Characteristic	Number of Families (millions)		Percent of Total	
	All Families	Poor Families	All Families	Poor Families
Total	47.0	9.3	100	100
Age of Head:				
14–24 years	2.5	.8	5	8
25–54 years	30.4	3.9	65	42
55–64 years	7.3	1.4	16	15
65 years and over	6.8	3.2	14	34
Education of Head:				
8 years or less	16.3	6.0	35	61
9–11 years	8.6	1.7	19	17
12 years	12.2	1.5	26	15
More than 12 years	9.3	.7	20	7
Sex of Head:				
Male	42.3	7.0	90	75
Female	4.7	2.3	10	25
Labor Force Status of Head:				
Not in Civilian Labor Force	8.4	4.1	18	44
Employed	36.9	4.6	78	49
Unemployed	1.7	.6	4	6
Color of Family:				
White	42.4	7.3	90	78
Nonwhite	4.6	2.0	10	22
Residence of Family:				
Rural Farm	3.3	1.5	7	16
Rural Nonfarm	9.9	2.7	22	30
Urban	31.9	5.0	71	54

Note: Data relate to families and exclude unrelated individuals. Poor families are defined as all families with total money income less than $3000.

Table 3

Number and Money Income of Unrelated Individuals, by Selected
Characteristics, 1962 [6]

Selected Characteristics	Number (millions)	Percent with Income	
		Less than $1,500 (1962 Prices)	Less than $1,000 (1962 Prices)
All Individuals	11.0	45	29
Age:			
14–24 years	1.1	51	40
25–54 years	3.5	27	19
55–64 years	2.3	37	25
65 years and over	4.2	64	37
Sex:			
Male	4.3	35	21
Female	6.8	51	34
Color:			
White	9.5	43	27
Nonwhite	1.5	59	41
Residence:			
Farm	.4	67	50
Nonfarm	10.6	44	28
Nonearners	4.3	75	49

Note: Unrelated Individuals are persons (other than inmates of
institutions) who are not living with any relatives. (C.E.A.
Report p. 79)

---

an aged person nor by a woman, and 70 percent include
at least one earner.[12]

—1.3 million poor families are headed by a white man who
was fully employed throughout the year.[13]

The incidence of poverty among households with employed
males is thus very high, contrary to public judgment, and ex-

tremely relevant to program strategy (as well as to causal explanations). For poor households headed by an employed male under sixty-five, the following data hold: [14]

Type of Family Head	*Percent of Employed Family Heads Living In Poverty, 1966*	
	Worked Full Year	*Worked Part Year*
White	3.9%	14.3%
Nonwhite	18.9%	36.4%

The existence of a large number of poor families headed by an employed male is a certainty. Orshansky highlights this point:

. . . in our work-oriented society, those who cannot or do not work must expect to be poorer than those who do. Yet, more than half of all poor families report that the head currently has a job. Moreover, half of these employed family heads, representing almost 30 percent of all the families called poor, have been holding down a full-time job for a whole year. In fact, of the 7.2 million poor families in 1963, 1 in every 6 (1.3 million) is the family of a white male worker who worked full-time throughout the year.[15]

The problem for these families is clearly one of inadequate wages, coupled with seasonal or temporary unemployment (a full-time job which does not last throughout the year—a category including another 1.5 million family heads). These families account for almost half of the families classified as being at or below the "poverty threshold." Herman P. Miller points out, "Although today's poor are frequently presented as psychologically or spiritually handicapped, the fact is that about 50 percent of them are headed by a full-time worker whose wages are simply too low to support a family." [16] The debilitating experience of being marginally employed is vividly portrayed in Tally's Corner,[17] a study of Negro streetcorner men in Washington, D.C. Given the work orientation of

American society, and the opprobrium cast upon those in
poverty, it is a bitter irony that full-time work at the minimum
wage of $1.60 per hour "produces an annual income of $3,200
for someone who works 40 hours per week, 50 weeks per year.
This is just about the poverty income threshold for a four-
person family. Workers who are paid less than the minimum,
or who receive the minimum wage but have families with
more than four members, are in poverty." [18]

Appendix B

Of the 310 American cities with a population of 50,000 or more, a "study population" of 79 cities was selected on the basis of two criteria:

1. had a funded Community Action Program grant other than summer Headstart as of June 30, 1965
2. is not New York or Los Angeles (which were considered too large).

These 79 cities were stratified by region according to whether they were in the:

1. Northeast-Central
2. Border
3. Southwest

Twenty cities were eliminated at this point for various reasons:

City	Reason for Dropping
1. Boston, Mass.	Our instrument Pre-test city
2. Baltimore, Md.	Overstudied
3. Norfolk, Va.	Not a city program
4. Washington, D.C.	Overstudied
5. Miami, Fla.	Not in Study Area
6. Tampa, Fla.	Not in Study Area
7. Atlanta, Ga.	Not in Study Area and Overstudied

City	Reason for Dropping
8. Chicago, Ill.	Too Large
9. Philadelphia, Pa.	Too Large
10. Detroit, Mich.	Too Large
11. Duluth, Minn.	Too Isolated
12. Racine, Wis.	Program Dropped
13. Austin, Tex.	Overstudied
14. Denver, Col.	Not in Study Area
15. Kansas City, Kan.	Overstudied
16. Ogden, Utah	Not in Study Area
17. Seattle, Wash.	Not in Study Area
18. Tacoma, Wash.	Not in Study Area
19. Portland, Ore.	Not in Study Area
20. Honolulu, Hawaii	Not in Study Area

The remaining 59 cities were each assigned a random number and stratified according to region. They stratified in the following pattern:

	Number	Fraction	Sample Size	Rounded
Northeast-Central	39	.6610	13.2	12
Border	9	.1527	3.1	4
Southwest	11	.1863	3.7	4
Total	59	1.0000	20	20

The Northeast was under-represented by one city in order to get an additional border state. Three border cities would have been too few to permit any generalizations.

Table 1 presents the mean values on variables used by Hadden and Borgatta [20] for four groups of cities; the parent population of all 310 American cities over 50,000 population; the study population 79; the study sample of 20; and the rejected 59 cities. No significant differences were found.

Table 1

Means of Groups

	1 Pop.*	2 %SDU	3 Density	4 Inc.	5 DI	6 %NW	7 %FB	8 Age	9 PI	10 %SH	11 %MI	12 Ec	13 CAP Mon.	14 Time
Parent Pop. (310)	227.0	3.8	5.0	4.4	5.1	5.1	4.9	4.8	4.2	4.6	4.1	4.9	—	—
Study Pop. (79)	338.4	3.0	5.9	3.8	6.3	6.3	5.5	5.2	3.0	5.1	3.1	4.8	—	—
Rejected (59)	361.2	2.7	6.1	4.0	6.1	6.6	5.6	5.4	2.8	5.1	3.2	5.1	—	—
Sample (20)	270.9	3.8	5.2	3.3	6.8	5.6	5.3	4.5	3.5	5.2	2.8	4.1	966.7	2.5

*Population in thousands
Variables 2–12 are H-B decile scores, range 0–9
The theoretical means for all 679 cities would be 4.5 for decile scores.

The means for the rejected group and the sample group were tested for significant differences by means of a series of one-way analyses of variance. None of the 12 H-B variables were found to be significantly different, thus confirming the hypothesis of the representativeness of the twenty cities with respect to the study population of seventy-nine.

NOTES

[1] Orshansky, Mollie, "Counting the Poor: Another Look at the Poverty Profile," in *The Social Security Bulletin*, Vol. XXVIII No. 1 (January, 1965), p. 5.

[2] Downs, Anthony, *Who Are The Urban Poor?*, Committee for Economic Development, 1968, pp. 1–2.

[3] Miller, Herman P., "Changes in the Number and Composition of the Poor," Margaret S. Gordon, ed., *Poverty in America* (San Francisco: Chandler Publishing Company, 1965).

[4] Council of Economic Advisers, *Annual Report to the President*, 1964.

[5] Council of Economic Advisers, *Report*, p. 61.

[6] *Ibid*, p. 79.

[7] Orshansky, "Counting the Poor: Another Look at the Poverty Profile," p. 5.

[8] *Ibid*, p. 5.

[9] *Ibid*, p. 5.

[10] Downs, *Who Are The Urban Poor?*, p. 3.

[11] *Ibid*, p. 3.

[12] Council of Economic Advisers Report, in *Monthly Labor Review*, Vol. LXXXVIII, No. 3 (March 1964), p. 289.

[13] Miller, "Changes in the Number and Composition of the Poor," p. 87.

[14] Downs, *Who Are The Urban Poor?*, p. 34.

[15] Orshansky, "Counting the Poor: Another Look at the Poverty Profile," p. 5.

[16] Miller, "Changes in the Number and Composition of the Poor," p. 87.

[17] Liebow, Elliot, *Tally's Corner* (Boston: Little, Brown & Co., 1967).

[18] Downs, *Who Are the Urban Poor?*, p. 34.

[19] Prepared by Kenneth J. Jones for the project staff, "Community Representation in Community Action Agencies."

[20] Hadden, Jeffrey K. and Borgatta, Edgar F., *American Cities: Their Social Characteristics*, (Chicago: Rand McNally, 1965).

Bibliography

Agger, Robert E., Goldrich, Daniel, and Swanson, Bert E. *The Rulers and the Ruled*. New York: John Wiley and Sons, 1964.

Banfield, Edward C. *Political Influence*. Glencoe, Ill.: The Free Press, 1961.

Briar, Scott. "Why Children's Allowances?". *Social Work*, Vol. 14 No. 1 (January, 1969).

Brown, Gordon E., ed. *The Multi-Problem Dilemma*. Matuchen, N.J.: Scarecrow Press, 1968.

Carmichael, Stokely, and Hamilton, Charles V. *Black Power: The Politics of Liberation in America*. New York: Vintage Books, 1967.

Clague, Ewan. "The Economic Context of Social Welfare in the United States." *Social Work Year Book—1957*. National Association of Social Workers: New York, 1957.

Clark, Kenneth B., and Hopkins, Jeannette. *A Relevant War Against Poverty: A Study of Community Action Programs and Observable Social Change*. New York and Evanston, Ill.: Harper and Row, Inc., 1969.

Cloward, Richard A., and Ohlin, Lloyd E. *Delinquency and Opportunity*. Glencoe, Ill.: The Free Press, 1960.

Community Welfare Council. *Report of the Multi-Problem Family Committee*. Family and Child Welfare Section. Rockford, Ill., 1958.

Coser, Lewis A. "The Sociology of Poverty." *Social Problems*, Vol. 13 No. 2 (Fall, 1965).

Council of Economic Advisers. Report of the Council. *Monthly Labor Review*, Vol. LXXXVIII No. 3 (March, 1964).

Council of Economic Advisers. *Economic Report of the President—1964*. Washington, D.C.: U.S. Government Printing Office, 1964.

Council of Social Agencies of Rochester and Monroe County. *Re-*

port on *Hard-to-Reach Multi-Problem Families.* Family and Children's Division. November 25, 1959.

Davidoff, Paul. "Advocacy and Pluralism in Planning." *Journal of the American Institute of Planners,* Vol. 31 No. 4 (November, 1965).

Davis, Allison. "The Motivation of the Underprivileged Worker," William Foote Whyte, *Industry and Society.* New York and London: McGraw-Hill Books Co., Inc., 1946.

Davis, Kingsley. "The Perilous Promise of Behavioral Science." *Research in the Service of Man: Biomedical Knowledge, Development and Use.* Washington, D.C.: Superintendent of Documents, 1967.

Dill, William R. "The Impact of Environment on Organizational Development," In: Sidney Mailick and Edward H. Van Ness, eds. *Concepts and Issues in Administrative Behavior.* Englewood Cliffs, N.J.: Prentice-Hall, Inc., 1962.

Donovan, John C. *The Politics of Poverty.* New York: Western Publishing Company, 1967.

Down, Anthony. *Who Are The Urban Poor?* Committee for Economic Development, 1968.

Durkheim, Emile. *The Rules of Sociological Method,* Translated by Sara Solovay, et al. New York: The Free Press, 1964.

Eckstein, Harry. *The English Health Service.* Cambridge: Harvard University Press, 1964.

Emery, S. E., and Trist, E. L. "The Causal Texture of Organizational Environments." *Human Relations,* Vol. 18 (February, 1965).

Etzioni, Amitai, ed. *Complex Organizations.* New York: Holt, Rinehart and Winston, 1964.

_____. *The Active Society: A Theory of Societal and Political Processes.* New York: The Free Press, 1968.

Evan, William M. "The Organization-Set: Toward a Theory of Interorganizational Relations," James D. Thompson, ed. *Approaches to Organizational Design.* Pittsburgh: University of Pittsburgh Press, 1966.

Frazier, E. Franklin. "Problems and Needs of Negro Children and Youth Resulting from Family Disorganization." *Journal of Negro Education.* (Summer, 1950).

Galbraith, John K. *The Affluent Society.* Boston: Houghton Mifflin Company, 1958.

Gamson, William A. "Stable Unrepresentation in American Society." *American Behavioral Scientist,* Vol. 12 No. 2 (November–December, 1968).

————. *Power and Discontent.* Homewood, Ill.: The Dorsey Press, 1968.

Gans, Herbert J. "Poverty and Culture: Some Basic Questions about Methods of Studying Life-Styles of the Poor." Paper presented at the International Seminar on Poverty, Essex University, April, 1967.

————. "Culture and Class in the Study of Poverty: An Approach to Anti-Poverty Research." In: Herbert J. Gans. *People and Plans: Essays on Urban Problems and Solutions.* New York: Basic Books, Inc., 1968.

Garfinkle, Irwin. "Negative Income Tax and Children's Allowance Programs: A Comparison." *Social Work,* Vol. 13 No. 4 (October, 1968).

Gerth, H. H., and Mills, C. Wright. *From Max Weber: Essays in Sociology.* New York: Oxford University Press, 1958.

Gil, David G. "Mothers' Wages: An Alternative Attack on Poverty." *Social Work Practice—1969.*

Graham, Elinor. "The Politics of Poverty," Ben B. Seligman, ed. *Poverty as a Public Issue.* New York: The Free Press, 1965.

Greer, Scott. *The Emerging City: Myth and Reality.* Glencoe, Ill.: The Free Press, 1962.

Grossman, David A. "The CAP: A New Function for Local Government," Bernard J. Frieden and Robert Morris, eds. *Urban Planning and Social Policy.* New York: Basic Books, Inc., 1968.

Hadden, Jeffrey K., and Borgatta, Edgar F. *American Cities: Their Social Characteristics.* Chicago: Rand McNally, 1965.

Harris, C. Lowell. "Statement on the Economic Opportunity Act of 1964," Burton A. Weisbrod. *The Economics of Poverty: An American Paradox.* Englewood Cliffs, N.J.: Prentice-Hall, Inc., 1965.

Hildebrod, George H. *Poverty, Income Maintenance, and the Negative Income Tax.* ILR Paperback No. 1. Ithaca, N.Y.: The Cornell University Press, 1968.

_____. "Second Thoughts on the Negative Income Tax." *Industrial Relations: A Journal of Economy and Society* (February, 1967).

Hill, Herbert. "Racial Inequality in Employment—The Patterns of Discrimination." *The Annals of the American Academy of Political and Social Science,* Vol. 357 (January, 1965).

Horowitz, Irving Louis. *Professing Sociology: Studies in the Life Cycle of a Social Science.* Chicago: Aldine Publishing Company, 1968.

Hunter, Robert. *Poverty.* New York: Macmillan Company, 1912.

Hyman, Herbert H. "The Value Systems of Different Classes." In: Reinhard Bendix and Seymour Martin Lipset, eds. *Class, Status and Power: Social Stratification in Comparative Perspective.* Second Edition. New York: The Free Press, 1966.

Keyserling, Leon H. "The Use of Social and Economic Resources to Eliminate Poverty." *Social Welfare Forum—1966.* New York: Columbia University Press, 1966.

Kravitz, Sanford L. "The Community Action Program—Past, Present, and Its Future." In: James L. Sundquist ed. *On Fighting Poverty.* New York: Basic Books, Inc., 1969.

Lampman, Robert J. "The Future of the Low-Income Problem." In: Burton A. Weisbrod. *The Economics of Poverty: An American Paradox.* Englewood Cliffs, N.J.: Prentice-Hall, Inc., 1965.

Larner, Jeremy, and Howe, Irving, eds. *Poverty: Views from the Left.* New York: William Morrow & Company, Inc., 1968.

Lefferts, Robert. "Pseudo-Policy: The American Approach to Housing." Unpublished paper.

Leighton, Alexander H. "Poverty and Social Change." *The Scientific American,* Vol. 212 No. 5 (May, 1965).

Lekachman, Robert. "Can 'More Money' End Poverty?". In: Jeremy Larner and Irving Howe, eds. *Poverty: Views from the Left.* New York: William Morrow & Company, Inc., 1968.

Levitan, Sar. *The Great Society's Poor Law: A New Approach to Poverty.* Baltimore: Johns Hopkins University Press, 1969.

Lewis, Hylan. *Perspectives on Poverty: A Study Manual.* Mimeographed.

————. "Agency Paper No. V: The Family: Resources for Change—Planning Session for the White House Conference 'To Fulfill These Rights'." In: Lee Rainwater and William L. Yancy. *The Moynihan Report and the Politics of Controversy*. Cambridge: The M.I.T. Press, 1967.

Lewis, Oscar. *Children of Sanchez*. New York: Random House, 1961.

————. *La Vida*. New York: Random House, 1966.

Liebow, Elliot. *Tally's Corner: A Study of Negro Streetcorner Men*. Boston: Little, Brown, and Company, 1967.

Lindeman, Edward C. *The Democratic Man*. Boston: Beacon Press, 1956.

Linton, Ralph. *The Study of Man*. New York: Appleton-Century-Crofts, 1936.

Long, Norton E. "The Local Community as an Ecology of Games." In: Norton E. Long. *The Polity*. Chicago: Rand McNally and Company, 1962.

————. "The Administrative Organization as a Political System." In: Sidney Mailick and Edward H. Van Ness. *Concepts and Issues in Administrative Behavior*. Englewood Cliffs, N.J.: Prentice-Hall, 1962.

————. "Community Decision-Making." *Community Leadership and Decision-Making*. University of Iowa Extension Bulletin No. 842.

————. "Power and Administration." In: Golembiewski, Robert T.; Gibson, Frank; and Cornog, Geoffrey, eds. *Public Administration*. Chicago: Rand McNally and Company, 1966.

Lumer, Hyman. *Poverty: Its Roots and Its Future*. New York: International Publishers, 1965.

Macarov, David. *Incentives to Work: The Effect of Unearned Income*. Unpublished Ph.D. Thesis, Florence Heller Graduate School for Advanced Studies in Social Welfare, Brandeis University, Waltham, Mass., 1968.

Machlup, Fritz. "Strategies in the War on Poverty." In: Margaret S. Gordon, ed. *Poverty in America*. San Francisco: Chandler Publishing Company, 1965.

Mailick, Sidney, and Van Ness, Edward H. *Concepts and Issues in Administrative Behavior*. Englewood Cliffs, N.J.: Prentice-Hall, Inc., 1962.

Mannheim, Karl. *Ideology and Utopia.* New York: Harcourt, Brace, and Company, Inc., 1936.

Marris, Peter, and Rein, Martin. *The Dilemmas of Social Reform.* New York: Atherton Press, 1967.

Matza, David. "The Disreputable Poor." In: Reinhard Bendix and Seymour Martin Lipset, eds. *Class, Status, and Power: Social Stratification in Comparative Perspective.* Second Edition. New York: The Free Press, 1966.

McKinney, John C. "Constructive Typology: Explanation of a Procedure." In: John T. Doby, ed. *An Introduction to Social Research.* New York: Appleton-Century-Crofts, 1967.

Mencher, Samuel. "Ideology and the Welfare Society. *Social Work,* Vol. XII No. 3 (July, 1967).

Merton, Robert K. *Social Theory and Social Structure.* Revised and Enlarged Edition. Glencoe, Ill.: The Free Press, 1957.

Meyerson, Martin, and Banfield, Edward C. *Politics, Planning and the Public Interest.* Glencoe, Ill.: The Free Press, 1955.

Miller, Herman P. "Changes in the Number and Compositions of the Poor." In: Margaret S. Gordon, ed. *Poverty in America.* San Francisco: Chandler Publishing Company, 1965.

Miller, S. M., and Rein, Martin. "Poverty and Social Change." *American Child,* Vol. XLVI No. 2 (March, 1964).

————, and ————. "The War on Poverty: Perspectives and Prospects." In: Ben B. Seligman, ed. *Poverty as a Public Issue.* New York: The Free Press, 1965.

————, and ————. "Participation, Poverty, and Administration." *Public Administration Review* (January–February, 1969).

Miller, Walter B. "Lower Class Culture as a Generating Milieu of Gang Delinquency." *Journal of Social Issues,* Vol. XIV No. 3, (1958).

————. "Implications of Urban Lower-Class Culture for Social Work." *Social Service Review,* Vol. XXXIII No. 3 (September, 1959).

Mills, C. Wright. *The Power Elite.* New York: Oxford University Press, 1959.

Mobilization for Youth, Inc. A Proposal for the Prevention and Control of Juvenile Delinquency by Expanding Opportunities. New York, 1961.

Montgomery, George W. "Reaching the Hard Core Family." Paper presented at the New York State Welfare Conference. Rochester, New York, 1957.

Morgan, James N., et al. *Income and Welfare in the United States.* New York: McGraw-Hill, 1962.

Moynihan, Daniel P. *Maximum Feasible Misunderstanding.* New York: Arkville Press, 1969.

_____. "What is Community Action?". *The Public Interest,* No. 5 (Fall, 1966).

Myrdal, Gunnar. "The War on Poverty." In: Arthur B. Shostak and William Gomberg, eds. *New Perspectives on Poverty.* Englewood Cliffs, N.J.: Prentice-Hall, Inc., 1965.

Nathan, Robert R. "Challenges to Our Affluent Society in Meeting Human Needs." *Social Welfare Forum—1966.* New York: Columbia University Press, 1966.

New York City Youth Board. *Reaching the Unreached Family: A Study of Service to Families and Children,* 1958.

New York State Charities Aid Association. *Multi-Problem Families: A New Name or a New Problem?,* May, 1960.

Nichol, Helen O. "Guaranteed Income Maintenance: Negative Income Tax Plans." *Welfare in Review,* Vol. IV No. 4 (April, 1966).

Niewenhuijze, C. A. O. Van. *Society as Process.* The Hague: Mouton and Company, 1962.

Office of Economic Opportunity. *Community Action Program Guide,* Volume I (February, 1965).

Oneida County Commissioners. *Community Development Program of Oneida County, Executive Director's Final Report,* June 30, 1959.

Orshansky, Mollie. "Counting the Poor: Another Look at the Poverty Profile." *Social Security Bulletin,* Vol. XXVIII No. 1 (January, 1965).

_____. "Measuring Poverty." *Social Welfare Forum—1965.* National Conference on Social Welfare. New York and London: Columbia University Press, 1965.

President's Commission on Income Maintenance Programs. *Poverty Amid Plenty: The American Paradox.* November 12, 1969.

Rainwater, Lee. "The Services Strategy vs. the Income Strategy." *Trans-action,* Vol. 4 No. 10 (October, 1967).

_____. "The Problem of Lower Class Culture." Pruitt-Igoe Occasional Paper No. 8—mimeographed.

Rein, Martin. "Social Science and the Elimination of Poverty." *Journal of the American Institute of Planners,* Vol. XXXIII No. 3 (May, 1967).

_____. "Poverty Programs and Policy Priorities." *Trans-action* (September, 1967).

_____. "Institutional Change: A Priority in Welfare Planning." In: Chaim I. Waxman, ed. *Poverty: Power and Politics.* New York: Grosset and Dunlap, 1968.

Report of the National Advisory Commission on Civil Disorders. Toronto and New York: Bantam Books, Inc., 1968.

Rodman, Hyman. "The Lower Class Value Stretch." *Social Forces,* Vol. 42 No. 2 (December, 1963).

Rose, Stephen M. "Schools and Social Reality." Paper presented at Annual Meeting of the Society for the Study of Social Problems, San Francisco, August 31–September 1, 1969.

Schattschneider, E. E. *The Semi-sovereign People.* New York: Holt, Rinehart & Winston, 1960.

Seligman, Ben B., ed. *Poverty as a Public Issue.* New York: The Free Press, 1965.

Selznick, Philip. *TVA and the Grass Roots: A Study in the Sociology of Formal Organizations.* Berkeley: University of California Press, 1953.

_____. "Critical Decisions in Organizational Development." In: Amitai Etzioni, ed. *Complex Organizations.* New York: Holt, Rinehart & Winston, 1964.

_____. "Foundations in the Theory of Organization." In: Amitai Etzioni, ed. *Complex Organizations.* New York: Holt, Rinehart & Winston, 1964.

_____. "Inherent Tendencies of Bureaucracies." In: William A. Glaser, and David L. Sills, eds. *The Government of Associations.* Totowa, N.J.: The Bedminster Press, 1966.

Shriver, R. Sargent. "Poverty in the United States—What Next?". *The Social Welfare Forum—1965.* National Conference on Social Welfare. New York and London: Columbia University Press, 1965.

Silberman, Charles E. *Crisis in Black and White*. New York: Random House, 1964.

Simmel, George. "The Poor." *Social Problems,* Vol. 13 No. 2 (Fall, 1965).

Sower, Christopher, et al. *Community Involvement*. Glencoe, Ill.: The Free Press, 1957.

Sundquist, James L. "Origins of the War on Poverty." In: James L. Sundquist. *On Fighting Poverty*. New York and London: Basic Books, Inc., 1969.

———. *On Fighting Poverty*. New York and London: Basic Books, Inc., 1969.

Sviridoff, Mitchell. "Contradictions in Community Action." *Psychiatry and Social Science Review,* Vol. 2, No. 10 (October, 1968).

Task Force on Urban Areas. *Preliminary Report—April 8, 1964.*

Thernstrom, Stephen. *Poverty, Planning, and Politics in the New Boston: The Origins of ABCD*. New York and London: Basic Books, Inc., 1969.

Thompson, James D. *Approaches to Organizational Design*. Pittsburgh: University of Pittsburgh Press, 1966.

———. *Organizations in Action*. New York: McGraw-Hill, 1967.

———. and McEwan, William J. "Organizational Goals and Environment: Goal-Setting as an Interaction Process." *American Sociological Review,* Vol. 23 No. 1 (February, 1958).

United States Commission on Civil Rights. A Report of the Commission. *A Time to Listen . . . A Time to Act*. Washington, D.C.: U.S. Government Printing Office, 1967.

United States Conference of Mayors. A Report of the Conference. Washington, D.C.: U.S. Government Printing Office, 1965.

United States Department of Health, Education, and Welfare. *Equality of Educational Opportunity*. Washington, D.C.: U.S. Government Printing Office, 1966.

United States Department of Labor. Office of Policy Planning and Research. *The Negro Family: The Case for National Action*. Washington, D.C.: U.S. Government Printing Office, 1965.

Valentine, Charles A. *Culture and Poverty*. Chicago: University of Chicago Press, 1968.

Vatter, Harold G. *The U.S. Economy in the 1950's: An Economic History.* New York: W. W. Norton & Company, Inc., 1963.

Walinsky, Adam. "Keeping the Poor in Their Place: Notes on the Importance of Being One-Up." In: Arthur B. Shostak and William Gomberg, eds. *New Perspectives on Poverty.* Englewood Cliffs, N.J.: Prentice-Hall, Inc., 1965.

Warren, Roland L. *The Community in America.* Chicago: Rand McNally and Company, 1963.

————. "Concerted Decision-Making in the Community." *The Social Welfare Forum—1965.* National Conference on Social Welfare. New York: Columbia University Press, 1965.

————, and Hyman, Herbert H. "Purposive Community Change in Consensus and Dissensus Situations." *Community Mental Health Journal,* Vol. 2 No. 4 (Winter, 1966).

————. "The Interaction of Community Decision Organizations: Some Basic Concepts and Needed Research." *Social Service Review,* Vol. 41 No. 3 (September, 1967).

————. "The Interorganizational Field as a Focus for Investigation." *Administrative Science Quarterly,* Vol. 12 No. 3 (December, 1967).

————. "Model Cities First Round: Politics, Planning and Participation." *Journal of the American Institute of Planners,* Vol. XXXV No. 4 (July, 1969).

Weber, Max. *The Methodology of the Social Sciences.* Edward A. Shils and Henry A. Finch, eds. Glencoe, Ill.: The Free Press, 1949.

Weisbrod, Burton A. *The Economics of Poverty: An American Paradox.* Englewood Cliffs, N.J.: Prentice-Hall, Inc., 1965.

Will, Robert E., and Vatter, Harold G., eds. *Poverty in Affluence.* New York: Harcourt, Brace & World, Inc., 1965.

Wilson, James Q. *Urban Renewal: The Record and the Controversy.* Boston: M.I.T. Press, 1966.

————. "An Overview of Centrally Planned Change." In: Robert Morris, ed. *Centrally Planned Change.* New York: National Association of Social Workers, 1964.

Wofford, John G. "The Politics of Local Responsibility—Administration of the Community Action Program, 1964–1966." In: James L. Sundquist, ed. *On Fighting Poverty.* New York: Basic Books, Inc., 1969.